The Musical Quest

An Adventure Through Sound

Jane Vera

Table of Contents

Introduction

Once upon a time, in a land far, far away, there existed a magical place called Harmonyland. It was a land where music wasn't just something you listened to; it was a part of the very air you breathed, the ground you walked on, and the sky above you. Imagine a place where the sun's rays created melodies as they touched the leaves, and the wind whispered harmonies through the tall grass.

So, close your eyes and picture a landscape where every tree, flower, and river hummed in perfect harmony. The hills rolled like gentle waves, creating a symphony of nature's own making. The mountains stood tall, conducting the clouds to form melodies that danced across the sky. Harmonyland was a masterpiece painted with the colors of music. Listen closely. Can you hear the soft hum of the grass beneath your feet? Feel the gentle breeze playing a tune with your hair. Look up, and you'll see birds singing notes that paint the air with vibrant hues. Harmonyland was a place where your senses could taste the sweetness of music in every breath.

Amidst this magical world, there's a spirited adventurer named Song. Song, the Musical Explorer, is a curious and lively guide who roams the enchanting landscapes of Harmonyland. She is a friend to all the creatures of this musical world and carries a magical instrument that can bring any melody to life. Song's eyes sparkle with excitement, and her heart beats in tune with the rhythm of Harmonyland.

Song's days are filled with the joy of discovering new musical wonders. She explores the hills, dances with the wind, and befriends the creatures that inhabit this harmonious kingdom. Song's enthusiasm for music is infectious, and she is always eager to share the magic of Harmonyland with others. But wait, the adventure is about to take an exciting turn! In the heart of Harmonyland, a musical challenge awaits Song and, of course, you! The challenge is to journey through the different musical realms and reach the grand castle in time for the spectacular music festival. The castle stands tall, its towers echoing with the promise of a melody that can unite all of Harmonyland.

As Song embarks on this thrilling quest, she invites you to join her. Together, you will encounter mysterious musical puzzles, face rhythmical riddles, and dance through melodic meadows. The journey won't be easy, but the reward of reaching the castle in time for the music festival is worth every musical step. But what's this? A sneak peek into the musical concepts that will accompany you on this adventure! Get ready to tap your toes to the rhythm, hum along with enchanting melodies, and discover the magic of harmonies. Rhythm, melody, and harmony will be your guides, leading you through a world where music is not just heard but felt in every fiber of your being.

Now, it's time for you to become an active part of this magical journey. Imagine yourself in Harmonyland, facing the challenges alongside Song. What musical mysteries will you unravel? Can you catch the tune of the wind or solve the riddles of the singing flowers? The adventure is as much yours as it is Song's. Think about it! As you journey through this musical tale, ponder the thought-provoking questions and challenges that pop up. What is the sound of a moonlit night? Can you imagine a forest where the trees whisper in perfect harmony? Your imagination is the key to unlocking the full magic of Harmonyland. And here's a little secret—this is just the beginning! There are hints of other musical realms, like the rhythmic Rhythm Kingdom and the melodic Melody Forest, waiting to be explored. But shh, we won't give away too much. The joy lies in discovering these magical places for yourself.

And so, with the sun setting on the horizon, casting a golden glow on your musical adventure, Song and her new companion (that's you!) set forth on a journey that would echo with the sounds of joy, discovery, and the magic that could only be found in Harmonyland. The castle awaited, and with each step, the melody became clearer, guiding you towards the grandest music festival in the land. So buckle up for a musical journey like no other.

Are you ready to unravel the mystery of the magical melody and explore the musical wonders of Harmonyland? The adventure has just begun!

Interactive Activity

Get ready for a musical adventure like never before! Join Song as she embarks on a journey through Harmonyland to discover the magical world of music.

Chapter 1:

The Rhythm Kingdom

Get ready to embark on a journey through the Rhythm Kingdom, where beats and notes dance to their own tune.

You will learn about note values, time signatures, and the heartbeat of music.

Introduction to the Rhythm Kingdom

Song arrives in the vibrant Rhythm Kingdom, a place where everything moves to a beat. As Song steps into this lively kingdom, she realizes that every sway of the trees, every step of its people, and even the flutter of butterfly wings follow a rhythmic flow.

In this enchanting land, rhythm is not just a part of the music—it is the very pulse that beats through the heart of Harmonyland.

Here, the wind whispers in syncopation, and the rivers flow with the rhythmic precision of a drumbeat.

The beautiful sounds of tapping feet fill the air, producing a dynamic symphony that resonates through the Rhythm Kingdom.

Here, rhythm forms the very essence of music, setting the stage for an exploration of its diverse elements.

Amidst this rhythmic wonderland, Song encounters a friendly musical note creature, Peter, a guide to the kingdom's secrets.

Together, they explore how rhythm forms the heartbeat of music, shaping the very essence of Harmonyland.

Peter explains how beats, like the kingdom's heartbeat, give life to music, setting the stage for a journey through various rhythmic elements.

All of this so amused her that she became curious about what rhythm is.

Interactive activity:

Hey, you! It's time to get creative and design "Your Rhythm Kingdom!" You should use your imagination to conjure up a unique world inspired by music. Whether through drawing or crafting, the idea is to visualize a vibrant realm where every element is infused with the essence of music.

Envision a 'beat river' symbolizing different rhythms flowing through your kingdom and 'note value trees' swaying in harmony with the melody. Allow yourself to bring to life a one-of-a-kind rhythmic wonderland that reflects your own creative expression and connection to music.

The Beat of the Land

In this lively kingdom, Song's eyes widen as she observes a captivating spectacle—everything, from the majestic trees to the playful animals, moves in perfect harmony with a steady beat. It's as if the entire kingdom dances to an invisible rhythm, each element synchronized like notes in a magical melody.

Curiosity gleams in Song's eyes as her guide, Peter, introduces her to the concept of musical beats.

To make learning about beats playful and interactive, Peter suggests an engaging activity that you can participate in too. Peter emphasizes that to understand a beat better, it is important to first grasp what rhythm is in music and defines it as the pattern of sound, silence, and emphasis in a song. Much like a heartbeat in the human body, a steady beat in music provides a regular and predictable pulse, creating a sense of rhythm.

To explain this concept further, Peter suggested an example of everyday sounds like the ticking of a clock. The consistent tick-tock creates a steady beat. This allows you to anticipate the next tick and establish a rhythmic pattern. Other examples can be some of the daily sounds, such as footsteps or the dripping of water from a faucet, which exhibit a steady beat, which can help you relate to the concept in music.

Interactive Activity: The Beat Discovery Walk

Take a walk, either inside or outside, and discover the natural rhythms that surround you. You can tap out these beats, matching them with claps or footfall, and discover the rhythms they create, whether it's the sound of footsteps, clock ticks, or faucet drips. This practice will assist you in connecting the abstract concept of a steady beat to the actual world, making rhythm in music learning a fun and immersive experience.

Dance of the Notes

As Song ventures deeper into the rhythmic wonders of the Rhythm Kingdom, she encounters a lively gathering of music notes. Each note, with its own unique personality, dances in captivating patterns, creating a mesmerizing visual symphony. Some notes twirl gracefully, while others bounce energetically, all contributing to the dance of the kingdom.

Inquisitive as ever, Song is drawn into the dance, eager to understand the secrets behind these enchanting movements. The notes, like cheerful companions, welcome her into their rhythmic world. Here, Song gets the opportunity to learn about the different notes and their note values—the duration and rhythm each note contributes to the music.

As Song steps onto the dance floor, she's welcomed by the whole musical ensemble: the whole notes, half notes, quarter notes, and eighth notes. Each note dances according to its note value.

First, the whole note, a round and complete character, begins the dance with a slow and graceful movement, taking up the entire stage. It represents four beats, holding its position with a serene presence.

Next up is the half note, a character that elegantly sways for two beats, filling the air with a delightful rhythm. Song mimics the movements, understanding how the half note's duration differs from the whole note, creating a sense of variation in the dance.

The quarter notes burst onto the scene, their lively and quick steps animating the dance floor with a sense of energy. Song, caught up in the excitement, follows suit, realizing that each quarter note represents one beat.

Then comes the eighth notes, twirling and dancing with twice the speed. Song's feet move swiftly to match their lively rhythm, understanding that each eighth note signifies half a beat.

Through this beautiful dance with the notes, Song comes to understand note values and how whole notes, half notes, quarter notes, and eighth notes contribute to music by defining its rhythmic structure. Whole notes represent long durations (four beats), half notes halve that time, quarter notes further divide, and eighth notes add intricacy.

Their combinations create rhythmic diversity, enhancing musical expression. As Song twirls with the notes, she internalizes the essence of musical timing.

Interactive activity

To make this exploration more interactive for you, not involved in Song's dance, you can instead engage in the "Rhythm Clapping Game." You can participate in this rhythmic adventure by clapping out simple patterns using different note values.

The challenge unfolds as you start with a slow pace, gradually increasing the speed. As Song moves from one note to another, you, too, can participate by clapping to the beats. Through this engaging activity, you will experience firsthand how various note values come together to create distinct rhythms, offering a playful and hands-on approach to understanding the magical language of music.

Time Signature: The Rhythm's Rule

Song's journey through the Rhythm Kingdom is interrupted by a mysterious challenge—a conundrum that demands she discover the secrets of time signatures in order to progress. As she approaches this musical conundrum, a puzzle delicately woven into the very fabric of the realm, the air is thick with expectancy.

In the heart of the challenge lies the concept of time signatures, the musical notation that organizes beats within a measure of time. The kingdom seems to pulse with a rhythmic energy, and Song understands that time signatures define how this pulse is measured in each bar. The tempo, or the speed of the pulse, further adds to the complexity of the challenge, determining the beats per measure.

The guide, Peter, explains the fundamental idea behind time signatures, using the most common one in music—4/4. The fraction-like symbol, with a four on top and a four on the bottom, signifies that there are four beats in one measure of time, and these beats are measured in terms of quarter notes.

This understanding forms the key to unlocking the puzzle, as Song realizes how the beats are organized within the measure, creating the rhythmic foundation of the music.

Beyond the common 4/4 time signature, there are many others, each adding a unique flavor to the musical landscape. From the waltz's 3/4 signature to the world of compound and odd time, Song discovers that time signatures are important in shaping the diverse rhythms found in the kingdom.

Interactive activity: Be the Conductor

As Song tackles the challenge, you can join in the adventure. You can immerse yourself in the world of 4/4 time by waving a baton to match the beat of a simple song. With synchronized conducting movements and counting aloud, you tend to physically connect with the rhythmic pulse.

As Song unravels the puzzle, you actively engage, moving to the beats of 4/4 time. The goal is to offer a sensory experience, allowing you not only to grasp the concept but also to physically participate.

Rhythm Patterns: Building Blocks of Music

Then, Song is challenged to create a rhythm pattern while on a musical quest, revealing hidden routes through the enchantment of musical composition. This task unfolds as a fascinating puzzle in which time signatures, notes, and beats come together to generate rhythmic sequences. Consider time signatures to be architectural blueprints, outlining the framework with fractions such as 4/4 indicating four beats per measure and the quarter note getting one beat.

Song had to use her knowledge of the time signature to guide her through this creative approach. By changing the note values—quarter notes, half notes, or whole notes—she learned that she could add new durations to the pattern. As she placed the different notes within the measure, she created rhythmic patterns that swung within the beats. She tried out different combinations of the note placements on the time signature.

Consider one of her simple 4/4 patterns: a quarter note on beat one, two eighth notes on beat two, a half note on beat three, and a quarter note on beat four. This basic sequence lays the rhythm's groundwork. Now, she also tried out the different possibilities by varying note values, adjusting placements, or introducing rests, which produced different rhythm patterns.

As Song is busy, you can also compose your own rhythm by utilizing a basic rhythm template featuring missing notes. Fill in the blanks with your chosen note values to craft a unique rhythm pattern. You can also try out a pattern with a whole note on beat one, a quarter rest on beat two, a half note on beat three, and a quarter rest on beat four.

The Pulse of Music

After passing the challenge, she progressed on her journey. In the heart of Harmonyland, she found herself in a lively concert, a pulsating celebration where rhythm takes center stage. From her guide, Song had to understand that rhythm is the heartbeat of music, establishing its pulse and infusing it with energy and movement. It is the organized pattern of sounds and silences within a musical composition that determines the arrangement of beats and accents.

The steady pulse generated by rhythm provides the foundation for musical timing, allowing listeners to connect emotionally and physically with the piece. Different note values, such as whole notes, half notes, quarter notes, and eighth notes, contribute to the intricacy of rhythm, dictating the duration and emphasis of each sound.

The rhythmic interplay between instruments or voices creates a dynamic sense of motion, which shapes the overall character of the music. Whether through syncopation, a deliberate disruption of the regular pulse, or through a consistent and driving beat, rhythm propels the listener through the musical journey, generating anticipation and excitement. In essence, rhythm is the life force that animates music, giving it a vibrant, pulsating quality that captivates and resonates with audiences across diverse genres and cultures.

In a jubilant celebration, Song triumphantly completes her task, setting the rhythm at the heart of the festivities. Her journey echoes your exploration: from the introduction of beats, the discovery of steady beats, a dance through different note values, a glimpse into time signatures, to crafting and recognizing rhythm patterns. As Song reflects on the significance of rhythm, it mirrors your own learning journey, concluding with the vibrant pulse of music resonating through Harmonyland.

Workbook Activity: Rhythm Kingdom

Activity 1: Coloring Beats
Color the different types of notes based on their values. Connect the dots to create rhythmic patterns.

Go to activity #1 in your workbook.

Activity 2: Beat Detective
Match notes to their corresponding time values and learn about different time signatures.

Go to activity #2 in your workbook.

Chapter 2:

The Melody Forest

Now, we will explore the enchanting Melody Forest, where tunes and melodies grow on musical trees. Discover the secrets of scales, intervals, and how to create your own musical melodies.

Welcome to The Melody Forest

As Song continues her exploration through the beautiful world of Harmonyland, she encounters a talking bird with a melodious trill, which becomes her guide. This mystical creature leads her into the enchanting Melody Forest, where melodies grow like living plants and are carried by the gentle wind. The forest itself is a symphony, with trees humming tunes, flowers chiming melodies, and the breeze whispering harmonious notes.

Each step Song takes in the Melody Forest contributes to a dynamic musical composition, with the vibrant surroundings resonating with various musical scales. The entire forest pulsates with rhythmic patterns, creating a living and breathing tapestry of melody.

In this musical haven, every element of nature, from the rustle of leaves to the songs of birds, becomes a valuable lesson in the art of melody. For her to navigate the forest with ease, she had to first understand that melodies are key in this adventure.

Interactive Activity: Create Your Forest Map

If you want to be involved with Song, you can draw a map of your unique Melody Forest, envisioning where musical elements like scales and intervals might reside. In this way, you can move along and enjoy this journey together with her.

Scales: The Building Blocks of Melody

Guided by the talking bird, Song explores unique areas in the forest, each representing a distinct musical scale. Musical scales are like the essential building blocks of melodies.

The guide goes on to say that scales are sequences of notes arranged in either ascending or descending order that serve as a structure for musical compositions.

She must realize that by understanding how these scales function, she will be able to compose more expressive, harmonic melodies that give music depth.

Musical scales are fundamental to understanding the tonal structure of the forest. Two primary types are major and minor scales. The major scale, recognized for its bright and uplifting sound, follows a specific pattern of whole and half steps. For instance, the C Major scale comprises the notes C, D, E, F, G, A, and B. Conversely, the minor scale exudes a more somber vibe, often associated with introspective or melancholic moods. The A Natural Minor scale includes the notes A, B, C, D, E, F, and G.

To understand this better, Song has to try to visualize a stream winding through the woods, mirroring the structured flow of a musical scale. The babbling water represents the seamless transition between notes, akin to a well-crafted melody. In this forest, nature itself is a living composition, showcasing how scales are the essence of melodies, shaping the very fabric of musical expression and giving form to the enchanting world of Harmonyland.

Interactive activity suggestion: Scale Scavenger Hunt

Use the following simple tunes:

1. **Twinkle, Twinkle, Little Star**

Notation: C-C-G-G-A-A-G

2. **Scarborough Fair**

Notation: E-D-C-D-E-C-E-F-G-A-B-A-G-F-E

3. **Happy Birthday**

Notation: C-C-D-C-F-E

Then, identify whether the tune is in a major or minor scale. This activity helps in understanding the sound and feel of different scales.

Intervals: The Steps Between Notes

After fully understanding the musical scales, Song comes across a series of musical puzzles or bridges that require an understanding of intervals to cross. Her guide has to help her throw more light on what intervals are. In this forest, the concept of intervals emerges as a musical ruler, measuring the distance between two notes—crucial for understanding the relationship and space between tones. Intervals are defined as the building blocks of melody and harmony, measured in scale degrees or semitones.

For easy understanding, the guide offered Song the forest grand piano. On the piano, the distance between adjacent keys illustrates different intervals. For instance, moving from C to D or from E to G represents specific intervals. The guide adds that understanding intervals is key in building chords, crafting melodies, and understanding the overall harmony in music. Examples include:

- **Minor Second (C-C#):** This interval creates tension and is often used for dramatic effect.

- **Major Seventh (C-B):** It brings a sense of longing or anticipation, contributing to a dreamy or contemplative mood.

- **Augmented Fourth/Diminished Fifth (C-F# or C-Gb):** Known as the tritone, it's dissonant and unsettling, frequently used for building tension and adding drama.

- **Perfect Octave (C-C):** Similar to a perfect unison, it adds a feeling of stability and unity but with a sense of elevation, often used for climactic moments.

In the magical forest, intervals take on a vibrant life. So just imagine birds contributing to the symphony of nature with calls that mirror these musical intervals. At dawn, a unison may resonate, while deep within the groves, a minor seventh may add a mysterious hue. These intervals become the colors of a living musical tapestry, which weaves a diverse and enchanting symphony in the forest.

Song, now armed with this knowledge, applies it to overcome these challenges to make the navigation of the forest even easier. At this moment, she understands how intervals are the key to this. Each solved puzzle becomes a harmonious step forward, illustrating the practical magic of intervals in the captivating Harmonyland.

Crafting Your Own Melody

In Song's enchanting journey, she is tasked with creating a melody to unveil a hidden forest path. Based on what she already knew about the essence of melodies, these musical creations (melodies) hinge on pitch and duration. Melodies come in three forms:

- **Chord-based melodies:** Originating from chord changes, utilizing chord tones for composition.

- **Scale-based melodies:** Comprising notes within a specific scale or mode, like a C major melody using notes from the C major scale.

- **Monotone melodies:** Essentially rhythmic patterns, found in some hip-hop vocals and EDM dance beats.

Guided by her guide, the talking bird, Song learns the structured art of melody crafting, which she does. After successfully creating her melody, she shares how she managed to make it. She says that she had to go through the following process:

1. **Choosing her instrument:**

   o She initiated the melody-creation process by selecting an instrument. Understand that different instruments can produce varied melodies, even when following the same chord progression.

2. **Selecting the key:**

   o She then identified the key based on the active chords, taking into account her vocal range and the ease of chord execution on her chosen instrument.

3. **Crafting chord progressions:**

   o She built a chord progression to serve as the cornerstone of her melody. This is imperative to record both the chords and their subtle nuances for future reference.

4. **Prioritize the chorus melody:**

   o Then, she channeled her creative energies into shaping the chorus, recognizing it as the pivotal and most memorable segment of her song. She had to develop a captivating, repetitive melody that formed the nucleus of her musical composition.

5. **Developing verse melodies:**

   o She progressed to creating the supporting elements, specifically the verses. Given that the chorus takes the spotlight, she felt liberated to experiment with more intricate and adventurous melodies in the verses.

The following are the tips she advises us to follow to create our own melodies:

- Start improvising on chord changes.

- Combine notes from major or minor scales.

- Write with a plan, considering chorus, verse, and pre-chorus melodies.

- Create focal points with high or low notes.

- Mix stepwise motion with occasional leaps.

- Repeat phrases, altering notes or rhythm slightly.

- Experiment with counterpoint, interweaving two melodies.

- Try writing away from your instrument, using a recorder app for vocal lines.

- Analyze and borrow techniques from your favorite artists' melodies.

Interactive Activity: Melody Maker

Based on the insights you have gained, you are about to create your own melody. You can use the clap-and-snap rhythm. To do this, start with a basic rhythm involving claps and snaps. For instance, try alternating between clapping your hands and snapping your fingers.

Experiment with the speed and pattern to find a rhythm that appeals to you. Once you have a steady beat, add simple notes using a piano or by humming to create your unique melody.

The Secret Language of Melodies

As Song ventures deeper, she discovers melodies that evoke different emotions; she may have noticed this in the areas in the forest that each represented a different scale. She learned that, at these scales, melodies possess a transcendent quality, communicating emotions and narratives beyond the limitations of language.

Through a meticulous arrangement of notes, they elicit a spectrum of feelings, utilizing pitch, rhythm, and dynamics as tools to paint emotional landscapes. Similar to how words form sentences, melodies string together musical phrases to convey stories without verbal expression.

The rise and fall of notes construct a dynamic journey, mirroring the ebb and flow of emotions. Whether triumphant or melancholic, melodies serve as protagonists, driving musical plots and engaging listeners emotionally. Across genres and compositions, melodies become universal storytellers, transforming abstract sentiments into shared experiences and highlighting their role as conduits connecting composers and listeners through the evocative language of music.

Simple melodies, like musical vignettes, hold emotional nuances and storytelling potential. By dissecting their composition—examining note progression, tempo, and tonality—you can unravel the emotional tapestry woven within. A gentle rise may signify hope, while a descending sequence hints at melancholy. These seemingly uncomplicated melodies are eloquent storytellers, conveying a rich array of emotions, proving that complexity isn't always required to evoke profound feelings and narrate captivating tales through the language of music.

With all that information at Song's fingertips, she was tasked with matching melodies with the right emotions or stories. All she had to do was listen and feel the melody, then describe the emotion it evoked. She could either draw or write down the emotions. This would help her learn how to connect emotions with musical sounds with ease.

Melodic Match Game

Song participates in a gathering, possible picnic, or bonfire party, where she plays a melody-matching game with other characters, and you are also invited to play along. This game invites players to match five distinct melodies with corresponding stories or scenes to advance the narrative.

- **Melody 1:** A light and playful tune with upbeat notes.

Which story or scene best suits this melody? Is it a cheerful day at a carnival, a lively gathering of friends, or the joyous celebration of a special achievement?

- **Melody 2:** A haunting and mysterious melody with eerie undertones.

Dive into the enigma of this melody. Does it accompany a suspenseful night in a haunted mansion, a secret rendezvous in a dimly lit alley, or the discovery of a hidden realm?

- **Melody 3:** A soothing and tranquil composition with gentle, flowing notes.

Picture the serenity of this melody. Is it a peaceful sunrise by the ocean, a quiet stroll through a serene forest, or a moment of introspection under a starry night sky?

- **Melody 4:** An intense and dramatic sequence with powerful crescendos.

Feel the intensity of this melody. Does it underscore a climactic battle between rivals, the emotional peak of a love story, or the decisive moment in a grand adventure?

- **Melody 5:** A whimsical and fantastical tune that sparks imagination.

Let your creativity flow with this melody. Is it the backdrop for a magical journey through a mystical realm, a fantastical encounter with mythical creatures, or a dreamlike exploration of an otherworldly landscape?

At the end of her journey through the Melody Forest, Song reflects on what she has learned about melodies. She has explored the foundational elements of musical expression—scales, intervals, and melody creation. Scales like major and minor provide harmonizing notes, while intervals shape emotional character through pitch relationships.

The methodical melody-crafting process, from choosing instruments to composing catchy choruses, offers a structured approach for budding composers. Reflecting on The Melody Forest's harmony, these elements converge into a vibrant symphony where diverse melodies, rhythmic rustles, and harmonious whispers create an enchanting musical landscape.

Song hints at the new musical concepts to expect in the next discovery in the upcoming chapter: the secrets of crafting compositions that resonate with The Melody Forest's essence in a symphonic journey.

Workbook Activity: Melody Forest

Activity 3: Melody Tree Maze
Guide Song through a maze of musical trees, identifying scales and intervals.

Go to activity #3 in your workbook.

Activity 4: Create Your Melody

Draw your own musical melody using the provided blank sheet. Use the knowledge gained in Melody Forest.

Go to activity #4 in your workbook.

Chapter 3:

Harmony Hills

At this point, you will climb the Harmony Hills and learn about chords, harmony, and the art of blending different musical notes together to create beautiful sounds.

Welcome to Harmony Hills

Song enters Harmony Hills, a colorful valley where all the elements are in perfect balance and the noises of the plants and animals blend together to create a symphony. Harmonious noises flood the air as each leaf adds a unique note to the ambient song. The advent of melody is greeted by a waterfall of melodic tones, and the lively surroundings respond melodically to each stride. The immersive soundscape captures Song's senses, sparking her curiosity and eagerness to unravel the secrets of harmony. The hills come alive with musical dialogues, and Song's inquisitive nature is piqued by the harmonious interplay of natural elements. This serene environment becomes the center for her next musical exploration, providing the groundwork for comprehending the intricate concept of harmony in music. In this valley, Song meets a harmonious character, a musical tree, who introduces her to the concept of harmony in music. This tree sets Song on a quest to understand and create harmony, adding a sense of adventure and purpose to her journey.

Interactive activity: Design Your Harmony Hill

Before we go any further, you should draw or craft your own version of Harmony Hills and include elements that symbolize harmony in music, such as intertwined vines for chords or flowing rivers for harmonious melodies.

This activity will ignite your imagination and set a creative tone for the chapter.

The Magic of Chords

As Song moves around, she discovers various chord flower gardens where different types of chords grow and blend. According to her guide, in the musical tree, chords are the vibrant bouquets that add richness and depth to the melodic landscape.

Her guide asks her to try and imagine a chord as a harmonious blend of different flowers, each representing individual musical notes that, when combined, create a beautiful arrangement.

Just as a flower garden is a collection of various blossoms, a chord is an amalgamation of individual notes played simultaneously. Imagine strolling through a musical garden and plucking individual notes like colorful petals from different flowers.

Each note carries its own unique sound, just like each petal has a distinct color and fragrance.

Then, she gathers a handful of these notes—petals—and places them together. Voila! She has formed a chord, a harmonious cluster that resonates with a unified sound. Her guide further explains that these chords are categorized into two basic chord types: the major and minor chords. The major chord is like a sunflower, radiating brightness and positivity.

In contrast, the minor chord mirrors the subtle beauty of a violet, with a touch of melancholy. Then, there is also a diminished chord—picture it as a delicate orchid, introducing an intriguing twist—while the augmented chord, resembling a blooming rose, adds a hint of tension and excitement.

Interactive activity

To experiment with creating or hearing chords, consider using a piano as your musical gardening tool.

Using the following simple guide showing how to play basic chords like C major, G major, and A minor, play these chords and take notice of the difference in sound and feeling between major and minor chords.

C Major Chord

- **Notes:** C, E, G

- **Finger placement:**

    o   Place your thumb (1) on C.

    o   Middle finger (3) on E.

    o   Pinky finger (5) on G.

- **Play:** Press all three keys simultaneously.

G Major Chord

- **Notes:** G, B, D

- **Finger placement:**

  o Put your thumb (1) on G.

  o Middle finger (3) on B.

  o Pinky finger (5) on D.

- **Play:** Press all three keys together.

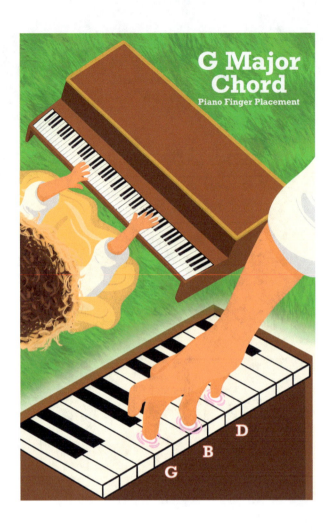

A Minor Chord

- **Notes:** A, C, E

- **Finger placement:**

    o   Place your thumb (1) on A.

    o   Middle finger (3) on C.

    o   Pinky finger (5) on E.

- **Play:** Press all three keys simultaneously.

Tips

- Keep your fingers curved and relaxed.

- Practice slowly at first, then gradually increase speed.

- Play each chord separately, then try transitioning between them.

This experience will help you understand the basic building blocks of harmony.

Harmony in Nature

Song comes across a section of the hills where the natural world reflects musical harmony, like a babbling brook that mimics a harmonious melody as it hits rocks on its journey. Her guide reveals how nature and music are interconnected through harmony. According to the guide, nature is a grand symphony of harmonious interactions where diverse elements synchronize to create mesmerizing melodies.

For instance, imagine the rhythmic rustling of leaves as a gentle breeze weaves through a forest. Each leaf, like a musical note, contributes to a harmonious composition. The synchronized chirping of crickets on a summer night is another exquisite example of nature's inherent harmony. Their rhythmic patterns blend seamlessly, forming a unified chorus that resonates through the air. These natural harmonies, whether in the rustle of leaves or the cricket's chirp, showcase the intricate interplay of elements, akin to musical notes coming together to create a cohesive melody.

Drawing parallels between natural harmonies and musical harmonies reveals the inherent musicality of the world around us. Harmonies can be seen in patterns found in nature, such as the rhythmic crashing of waves on a shoreline or the coordinated movements of a flock of birds. These patterns, much like musical chords, result from the interaction of individual elements.

Harmony in music compositions is the result of combining many musical notes at the same time to produce a pleasing sound. Similarly, in nature, the orchestrated combination of sounds produces a harmonious effect.

Nature's harmonies also reflect the principles of musical harmony, where certain combinations are perceived as more consonant or pleasant. For example, the harmonic series, a fundamental concept in music theory, is mirrored in the natural vibrations of elements like strings or air columns. Recognizing these parallels enhances our appreciation for the musicality ingrained in the world, demonstrating that harmony is not merely a human creation but an inherent aspect of the natural order.

To deepen her understanding through observation, Song is encouraged to listen to and describe the natural harmonies. She had to look around her surroundings to discover the different melodies. She had to also actively listen to the natural sounds around her, fostering an awareness of the harmonies present in her environment. Whether it's the rhythmic cadence of raindrops, the harmonious babble of a stream, or the wind's melodic whispers, nature provides an immersive auditory experience.

She had to identify patterns in these sounds, akin to musical harmony, then connect them to connect with nature on a deeper level. This would not only help her appreciate the different harmonies but also spark creativity by recognizing the parallels between the artistry of nature and the composition of music.

Interactive activity suggestion: Harmony Hunt in Nature

In order for you to deepen your understanding, just like Song, go on a 'harmony hunt' in your backyard, local park, or around your home, listening for natural sounds that create harmony. Then, describe them in a journal, relating each to musical harmony. This will help you connect the concept of harmony with your everyday experiences.

Creating Harmonies

Song is tasked with creating a harmonious melody to calm a chaotic part of the forest. But she must understand that the essence of harmony lies in artfully combining different notes to produce a pleasing auditory experience. Similar to the way the Harmony Hills resonate with the graceful interplay of leaves and breezes, achieving musical harmony requires the intricate blending of individual notes. She has to start by grasping the fundamental concept of intervals, as discussed in the previous chapter, commonly categorized as thirds, fourths, and fifths.

Her guide has to help guide her through this process of creating harmony. This process involves delving into basic music theory. First, she can harmonize a melody by incorporating notes that construct chords. For instance, if the melody features a C note, harmonizing it entails adding an E note (a third above) to create a harmonious blend. So, her guide encourages her to experiment with harmonizing different segments of the melody, which requires her to understand the significance of chord progressions in relation to the melody's key. Common harmonies often revolve around major or minor chords that complement the melody's tonality.

As we join Song in crafting a short melody, initiate with a simple, memorable tune. Following the melody's establishment, engage in experimentation by introducing harmonious notes. In the context of a C major melody, experimenting with harmonization could involve adding E and G notes, forming a harmonious chord progression. The key lies in attentive listening to discern how the added notes enhance the overall auditory experience. In harmony with Song's venture into The Harmony Hills, you are encouraged to embark on your harmonious journey, exploring the enchanting harmonies where each note contributes to the captivating musical landscape. Just as Song unravels the secrets of harmony within the natural sounds of The Harmony Hills, you can also unlock your harmonious potential within your musical creations.

Harmony in Songs

Song then comes across and listens to a choir of hill creatures, analyzing how their harmonious singing enhances the song. She discovered that harmony in music is a deciding element that elevates songs, adding layers and depth to the auditory experience. It involves the simultaneous combination of different notes, enriching the sonic landscape and providing a sense of fullness. Harmonies can convey emotions, emphasize specific moments, and enhance the overall impact of a musical composition.

The musical tree invites Song to identify harmonies in the choir's songs, making the learning process interactive and enjoyable. To illustrate the impact of harmony, consider iconic songs that showcase its significance. The Beatles' "Let It Be" features harmonious backing vocals that complement the lead melody, creating a rich and emotionally resonant sound. In Simon & Garfunkel's "Bridge Over Troubled Water," the harmonious interplay between Paul Simon and Art Garfunkel contributes to the song's powerful and comforting atmosphere.

Now, try to listen to a specific song together—Adele's "Someone Like You." As you analyze this poignant ballad, pay attention to the harmonies in the background vocals that enhance the emotional intensity of Adele's lead melody. The harmonious elements in this song exemplify how carefully crafted harmonies can evoke deep emotions and elevate the impact of a musical piece. This analysis allows you to actively engage with the concept of harmony, recognizing its transformative role in creating memorable and emotionally charged songs.

In Song's exploration of Harmony Hills, she unravels the secrets of harmony, understanding how chords weave the rich tapestry of music. Engaging with the characters in harmonious symphony, she celebrates the beauty of musical harmony, each encounter contributing to her newfound knowledge. Now, as Song prepares to depart from Harmony Hills, she anticipates her next destination, where the magical scenery mimics the unpredictable nature of the desert. There, she will explore the significance of tempo in music, navigating through a constantly shifting range of speeds and rhythms as she sets out on a rhythmic adventure through Harmonyland's rhythmic delights.

Workbook activity: Harmony Hills

Activity 5: Chord Connect-the-Dots
Connect musical notes to reveal hidden chords and learn how harmony is created.

Go to activity #5 in your workbook.

Activity 6: Blend It Right!
Color the harmony blend of different musical notes to create a harmonious landscape.

Go to activity #6 in your workbook.

Chapter 4:

Tempo Desert

It's now time to trek through the Tempo Desert, where the speed of music is as unpredictable as a sandstorm. You are going to understand tempo, dynamics, and how they shape the mood of a musical piece.

Entrance to the Tempo Desert

Song finds herself at the edge of a vast, ever-changing desert—the Tempo Desert—where the pace of life shifts from one extreme to the other. This desert is an expansive place where the very essence of music—the tempo—mirrors the ever-changing rhythm of shifting sands. As Song ventures into this desert, the environment itself is a symphony of diverse tempos, ranging from the slow, deliberate movements of colossal dunes to the quick, swirling currents of sands caught in a breeze. Each step echoes a different beat, immersing Song in the dynamic pulse of the desert. Here, tempo isn't just a musical concept; it's the heartbeat of this place. This desert is a living metaphor, where the sands of time dance to the ever-shifting rhythm, and Song stands poised to unravel the secrets of tempo in Harmonyland.

In her exploration, Song encounters a musical sandman who becomes her guide, introducing her to the intriguing concept of tempo. The sandman becomes Song's mentor, propelling her on a quest to unravel the mysteries of tempo and its profound influence on the world of music in Harmonyland.

The journey into Tempo Desert marks the beginning of a rhythmic adventure where you and Song will navigate through varying speeds, mirroring the nuanced tempo shifts that characterize the musical world.

Interactive Activity: Desert Rhythm Drawing

Before going deep into the desert, draw your interpretation of Tempo Desert, incorporating elements that represent different tempos (e.g., slow-moving rivers for adagio, fast-flying birds for allegro). This would give you a better understanding of what we are about to face.

Understanding Tempo

As Song ventures deeper, she encounters various 'tempo zones' in the desert, each representing a different tempo marking. Her guide explains to her the meaning of each tempo term and how it relates to the rhythm of the environment. Tempo, as defined by the guide, is the speed or pace at which a musical composition is performed in order to express rhythmic structure and a sense of time. The number of beats in a 60-

second period is shown by the measurement, which is beats per minute (BPM). The tempo sets the overall feel of a musical piece and can greatly influence its mood and emotional impact.

The common tempo terms include:

- **Largo**: Very slow and broad.

- **Andante**: At a walking pace, moderately slow.

- **Allegro**: Fast, quick, and lively.

- **Presto**: Very fast and brisk.

The guide adds, "These terms provide musicians with a standardized way to communicate the desired speed of a composition. For example, an Allegro tempo suggests a lively and fast-paced piece, while Largo indicates a slow and expansive movement."

In "The Tempo Desert," various areas represent different tempos. A Largo section is a vast expanse where everything moves slowly, creating a sense of solemnity and contemplation. Contrastingly, an Allegro section is a bustling and dynamic region characterized by rapid movement and energy. These shifts in tempo create a diverse and engaging musical terrain, guiding the listener through a range of emotional experiences within a single composition. The deliberate manipulation of tempo is a powerful tool for composers and performers to craft nuanced and expressive musical narratives.

Interactive Activity: Metronome Exploration

Materials Needed:

- Music player or any device to play music

- Various objects for tempo representation (e.g., soft toys, balls)

- Large space for movement

Instructions:

1. **Introduction (5 minutes):** Start with a brief explanation of tempos in music, using simple language. Discuss terms like "fast," "slow," and "medium" tempo.

2. **Tempo sorting (10 minutes)** Play different music tracks with varying tempos. Use objects representing different tempos (e.g., soft toys for slow,

balls for fast). Then match the objects with the tempo of the music you hear.

3. **Body movement (15 minutes):** Demonstrate how body movements can represent different tempos. Practice moving to the beat of the music. Use slow, flowing movements for slow tempos and quick, energetic movements for fast tempos.

4. **Musical statues (10 minutes):** Play music randomly, alternating between different tempos. When the music stops, freeze in a pose that represents the tempo you feel. Try to be creative in your poses.

5. **Tempo story (15 minutes):** Gather your friends and divide them into small groups, and assign each group a tempo (fast, slow, or medium). Ask them to create a short story or scene using their bodies to express the assigned tempo. Each group performs their mini-drama for the others.

6. **Interactive tempo art (10 minutes):** Provide art supplies (paper, markers, crayons) and then create visual representations of different tempos. This could include drawing lines, shapes, or patterns that reflect the mood of the tempo.

7. **Closing jam session (5 minutes):** End the activity with a jam session where you can use your bodies and objects to create a collaborative rhythm, combining different tempos. Celebrate your creativity and newfound understanding of tempos in music.

This will help you understand how tempo is measured and experienced.

The Beat of the Desert

In the Tempo Desert, Song keenly observes the desert's inhabitants, from elusive creatures to resilient plants, moving in sync with the rhythmic beat of the environment. She discerns how the tempo affects their energy and mood, analogous to the emotional impact of music's tempo variations. As the tempo shifts from slow and contemplative, mirroring vast, unhurried dunes (Largo), to brisk and lively, resembling the energetic dance of swiftly shifting sands (Allegro), Song recognizes the transformative power of tempo in shaping emotions.

Engaging in a meaningful conversation with the Desert Character, Song discusses the profound emotional influence of tempo changes in the rhythms. The character tells Song that these tempo variations play a role in altering the mood of a musical piece. Slow tempos induce a calm and reflective atmosphere, mirroring the stillness of a serene desert panorama. On the other hand, faster tempos inject vibrancy and excitement into the music, emulating the dynamic energy of a desert in motion.

The deliberate choice of tempo becomes a powerful tool for composers, enabling them to shape the emotional landscape of their compositions, much like the ever-changing emotions experienced in the diverse terrain of a desert. This relatable comparison between the dynamic shifts in music and the varied emotions evoked by the desert's terrain deepens Song's understanding and connects you to the emotional essence of tempo.

To understand this better, Song moves at different speeds, feeling how tempo changes alter her perception of the music.

Interactive Activity: Emotional Tempo

Play and listen to music clips with distinctly different tempos. Then, identify the mood each tempo sets. This will help you connect tempo with its emotional impact on music.

Navigating Rhythmic Sandstorms

Song faces challenges in the desert where the tempo suddenly changes, like a sandstorm that accelerates or a slow-moving fog. To overcome these challenges, she has to first understand how these changes came about. Her guide explains how these changes are similar to shifts of tempo in music, providing practical examples and teaching her how to adapt to the shifting rhythms of the desert storm. According to the guide, within a musical composition, tempo variations are analogous to the sudden and dramatic changes in the winds of a desert. Just like in a serene desert environment where, unexpectedly, a gust of wind sweeps through, altering the pace of the surroundings. Similarly, in music, abrupt shifts in tempo can introduce a sense of unpredictability and excitement.

In musical terminology, the gradual speeding up or slowing down of tempo is known as accelerando and ritardando, respectively. Accelerando, denoted as "accel.," instructs musicians to gradually increase the tempo, infusing the piece with a sense of urgency and momentum. This can be likened to the winds of the desert picking up speed, transforming the once calm atmosphere into a whirlwind of activity.

Conversely, ritardando, indicated as "rit.," directs performers to gradually decrease the tempo, creating a decelerating effect. This mirrors the calming of the desert winds, gradually settling back into a tranquil state. These nuanced changes in tempo allow musicians to convey a spectrum of emotions within a piece.

The musical term rubato, meaning "robbed" in Italian, allows for expressive flexibility in tempo. It permits the performer to temporarily speed up or slow down certain passages, creating a sense of freedom and emotional depth. This can be compared to the intermittent gusts or lulls in the desert wind, enhancing the musical narrative with a touch of spontaneity.

In essence, the desert's winds and music's tempo changes share a parallel of unexpected shifts. Understanding and manipulating these tempo variations provide composers and performers with a palette of expressive tools to craft a dynamic and emotionally resonant musical experience.

Song must navigate these challenges by adjusting her pace, demonstrating how tempo changes are managed. She then uses her new understanding of tempo dynamics to successfully find her way through the storm.

Interactive Activity: Tempo Change Dance

Create a fun dance or movement activity where you change your movement speed according to tempo changes in a real piece of music. Include moments of speeding up and slowing down in the musical choice to mimic the sandstorm's shifting tempos. This exercise will help you physically experience, understand, and connect to tempo changes.

The Mood of Music

In a calmer part of the desert, Song listens to music emanating from the environment, noting how different tempos evoke different genres and moods. In different parts of the Tempo Desert, Song experiences areas that represent various musical genres, each with its own characteristic tempo, contributing to the unique identity and mood of each style. In the Tempo Desert, Song encounters diverse musical landscapes that mirror the tempos associated with different genres, showcasing the rich variety in musical expression.

1. **Dance Oasis (Fast Tempo):** MSong stumbles upon a vibrant oasis where quick, pulsating beats resonate, creating an energetic dance atmosphere reminiscent of fast-paced electronic dance music (EDM) or techno genres. The lively tempo propels the desert's inhabitants into an exhilarating rhythmic dance.

2. **Serenade Springs (Slow Tempo):** Venturing into Serenade Springs, Song discovers a tranquil oasis with slow, flowing rhythms. The languid pace of the desert's musical waters mirrors the contemplative nature of ballads or slow jazz, creating a serene and introspective ambiance.

3. **Rock Ridge (Moderate Tempo):** Climbing the rocky terrains of Rock Ridge, Song encounters a steady, moderate tempo, echoing the resilience and energy characteristic of rock music. The rhythmic beat of the desert's stones aligns with the pulse of classic rock or alternative genres.

4. **Folk Foothills (Varied Tempo):** In Folk Foothills, Song experiences a varied tempo that mirrors the eclectic nature of folk music. The shifting rhythms reflect the diverse influences and storytelling traditions found in folk genres worldwide.

5. **Ambient Dunes (Ambient Tempo):** Song traverses the Ambient Dunes, where the music unfolds at a soothing and ambient tempo. This musical environment resonates with ambient genres, creating an immersive sonic experience that seamlessly blends with the desert's calm and expansive atmosphere.

She learns how tempo contributes to the mood and style of these genres making connections to real-world music.

Interactive Activity: Genre Tempo Match

Get a list of different music genres and the typical tempos associated with them. Then match the genres with their corresponding tempos, exploring how tempo helps define the character of each genre. I believe that this activity will enhance your understanding of how tempo is used in various musical contexts.

In conclusion, Song reflects on her experiences in The Tempo Desert, reflecting on everything she learned about tempo, music dynamics, and how they shape the mood of a musical piece. She realizes how tempo can dramatically alter the experience of music.

Workbook Activity: Tempo Desert

Activity 7: Sandstorm Dynamics
Color in a musical piece based on dynamic markings and understand how they shape the mood.

Go to activity #7 in your workbook.

Activity 8: Tempo Tracker
Match instruments to their appropriate tempos and learn about the dynamics of music.

Go to activity #8 in your workbook.

Chapter 5:

Instrument Isles

Sail to the Instrument Isles and meet the musical inhabitants, who play a variety of instruments. Learn about the families of instruments, their unique sounds, and how they come together in an orchestra.

Arrival at the Instrument Isles

Song arrives at a visually stunning archipelago where each island echoes with unique musical sounds. Her excitement and curiosity set the tone for exploration. Song is greeted by a talking butterfly who explains the concept of the Instrument Isles and prepares her for the journey ahead.

As Song stepped onto the first island, her eyes widened with excitement. Violins, cellos, and double basses harmonized like a celestial choir, welcoming her into the string family. The air was alive with the resonance of plucked and bowed strings, resonating with the elegance of centuries-old compositions.

Moving to the next island, the brass family revealed its bold and majestic spirit. Trumpets heralded Song's arrival, trombones resonated with deep richness, and French horns serenaded her with their warm embrace.

Each step led her to a new realm of musical discovery, with woodwinds inviting her to join their airy dance and percussion instruments urging her to feel the heartbeat of the archipelago.

Song marveled at the diversity, realizing that each island held unique insights into the world of instruments. The archipelago became her musical playground, a place where knowledge and harmony intertwined. Each family of instruments contributed to the symphony of the archipelago, and Song eagerly immersed herself in the rich tapestry of sound, unlocking the secrets of the islands one note at a time.

Interactive Activity: Isle Map Creation

According to the journey Song moved along, draw or design your map of the Instrument Isles, depicting different islands for various instrument families. This activity will help you set the scene and engage your imagination from the start.

String Island

The first island that Song explores is String Island. She marvels at the sounds of various string instruments and observes how they are played.

She sees demonstrations that illustrate how strings vibrate to produce music, perhaps through an interactive exhibit or a mini-concert by island inhabitants. This caught her attention. Her guide, the talking butterfly, had to explain to her how the island of string instruments operated to produce the beautiful sound. First, she had to learn about what string instruments are. The guide explained that string instruments like the violin, cello, guitar, and harp share common physical characteristics despite their distinct designs.

Each comprises a resonating body, typically wooden, which amplifies sound. The instruments feature a set of strings stretched tightly across a hollow cavity, with the tension of these strings crucial to producing the desired pitches. The violin and cello are members of the violin family, which is characterized by four strings and a curved, hollow body. The guitar, part of the guitar family, often has six strings and a flat or slightly curved body. The harp, distinctively, has multiple strings of varying lengths attached to a frame.

After learning about what these instruments are, she had to delve into how they are able to produce their unique sounds. And this is what her guide had to teach her. Sound production in string instruments results from the vibration of strings. Musicians initiate vibrations through techniques like plucking, bowing, or strumming. When a string is set into motion, it displaces air particles, creating sound waves. The hollow body of the instrument acts as a resonator, enhancing and projecting the sound. The length, thickness, and tension of each string determine its pitch.

Changing the length (by pressing on the fingerboard) or tension of the strings alters the pitch, allowing musicians to produce a range of notes. The bow in bowed instruments like the violin creates sustained vibrations, while plucked or strummed instruments like the guitar generate shorter, percussive sounds. The rich and diverse tones produced by string instruments contribute to their widespread use in various musical genres and cultural traditions.

Song was so excited to learn about all this that she decided to pick out a few of the instruments to practically exercise what she had learned.

Interactive Activity: String Instrument Sound Investigation.

In order to reinforce what you have learned about string instruments, visit your nearest music studio. Then try your best to identify the different instruments by how they sound.

Woodwind Island

As Song continued to the Woodwind Island, she encountered musicians playing woodwind instruments, each demonstrating the unique sounds they produce. She was fascinated by this. She asked her guide to try to explain to her about the woodwind instruments, just like she did with the string instruments. She really wanted to know how blowing air into these instruments creates their melodious sounds.

Her guide had this to say:

Delving into instruments like the flute, clarinet, oboe, and saxophone unveils a diverse world of woodwind musicality. The flute, a non-reed instrument, produces sound when the player blows across the mouthpiece's edge, causing air to split against the sharp edge, creating vibrations.

Known for its bright and clear tones, the flute is often featured in classical, jazz, and even folk music. The clarinet, with its single-reed mouthpiece, generates sound as the vibrating reed interacts with the instrument's body. Its versatile tonal range allows it to transition seamlessly between registers, making it a staple in orchestras and various genres.

The oboe, distinct for its double reed, requires a precise embouchure to produce its unique and piercing tones. Its timbre adds richness to classical ensembles. Lastly, the saxophone, with its brass body and single reed, spans a wide range of genres, offering a soulful sound in jazz and a powerful presence in rock.

Blowing air into woodwinds is a fundamental aspect of their sonic production. The player's breath, channeled through the instrument, interacts with the reed or edge to create vibrations. Reeds, commonly made from cane, are pivotal components. In clarinets and saxophones, a single reed vibrates against the mouthpiece, while oboes employ a double reed setup. The reed's material and thickness profoundly impact the instrument's tonal characteristics.

Understanding the interplay of breath, reed, and instrument construction provides insight into the nuanced world of woodwind instruments, each with its own distinct sonic footprint.

Interactive Activity: Make Your Own Woodwinds

Let's make our own paper flute. To make a simple paper flute, start by rolling a piece of paper tightly into a cylinder, securing it with tape. Leave one end open and flatten the other to create a mouthpiece. Cut a small rectangle near the flattened end to act as a sound hole. Attach a strip of paper or a drinking straw as a mouthpiece extension. Experiment with finger placement along the cylinder to create different pitches. Adjust the size of the sound hole for tonal variations. While this rudimentary paper flute won't match the sophistication of professional instruments, it offers a fun and accessible introduction to basic wind instrument principles.

Brass Island

Soon, Song arrives at Brass Island, where the sounds are bold and resonant. She learns about the mechanics of brass instruments from the island's musicians. The trumpet, trombone, French horn, and tuba constitute the most common members of the brass family, each possessing unique designs that contribute to their distinct sounds. The trumpet, with its cylindrical tubing and flared bell, produces a bright, piercing tone.

The trombone features a sliding mechanism, allowing players to change pitch smoothly. The French horn, recognized for its coiled shape, yields a warm and mellow sound. Tuba, characterized by its large size and conical tubing, produces deep, resonant tones.

These instruments play crucial roles in various musical genres, from orchestral compositions to jazz and marching bands.

Her guide demonstrates the concepts of embouchure and breath control to her. The guide explains that brass musicians employ a combination of breath control and embouchure, the manipulation of facial muscles around the mouthpiece, to produce sound. Controlled breathing facilitates the sustained airflow required for playing brass instruments, influencing dynamics and expression.

The embouchure, a player's lip and facial muscle formation, determines pitch and tone quality. Musicians master the delicate balance of lip tension, airspeed, and tongue placement for precision in articulation and intonation. Brass players often undergo rigorous training to develop endurance, ensuring consistent sound production. This intricate interplay of breath control and embouchure mastery is essential for musicians to unlock the full expressive potential of brass instruments. This challenges Song to try one out to feel the experience.

Interactive Activity: Brass Breath Control

You can now learn some breath control techniques. Brass players refine their breath control with a simple yet effective exercise using balloons. Inflate a balloon, emphasizing slow, controlled exhalation to ensure a steady stream of air. Focus on filling the balloon with a consistent, gentle breath, avoiding rapid bursts.

This mirrors the sustained airflow needed for brass instruments. Practice prolonged exhalation, gradually extending the duration, to build endurance. Additionally, balloon exercises encourage diaphragmatic breathing, expanding the lower lungs for optimal air support. Regular practice of these techniques enhances a brass player's ability to sustain long, controlled phrases and produce rich, resonant tones. With this activity, you can experience how breath control affects sound, mimicking brass instrument play.

Percussion Island

On Percussion Island, Song discovers a wide range of percussion instruments and learns about rhythm and beat. The beautiful creatures on this island engage Song in a rhythmic jam session or a fun percussion workshop, showcasing various percussion sounds and techniques. But first, they had to teach her about these instruments. They demonstrate the versatility and fun of percussion instruments.

She learned that percussion instruments form a vibrant and diverse family that includes drums, xylophones, and cymbals. Drums, with their varying sizes and materials, produce rhythmic beats, while xylophones contribute melodic elements with their tuned wooden bars. Cymbals, made of metal alloys, add a shimmering quality to the ensemble.

Each instrument possesses unique characteristics, contributing to the rich tapestry of percussive sounds. Drums, ranging from the deep resonance of the bass drum to the sharp snare drum, offer a wide tonal spectrum. Xylophones, with their distinct pitches, enhance musical expression. Cymbals, with crashes and sizzles, inject dynamic textures.

She further learned that percussion instruments play a vital role in shaping rhythm and adding texture to music. They create a rhythmic foundation, establishing the heartbeat of a composition. Drums set the pace, providing the pulse that guides other musicians. Xylophones, with their distinct notes, contribute to the overall melody, adding complexity to the arrangement. Cymbals punctuate and accentuate musical phrases, creating excitement and drama.

The ensemble of diverse percussion instruments collaborates to form intricate rhythmic patterns, enhancing the overall musical experience. From the driving force of a drumline to the delicate nuances of a vibraphone, percussion instruments showcase the breadth of sonic possibilities and remain essential contributors to the rhythmic landscape of various musical genres.

Interactive Activity: DIY Percussion Ensemble

Create a mini-percussion ensemble using your household items (pots, pans, boxes, etc.) Then use the beats and melodies made in previous chapters or experiment with creating new ones, exploring the variety of sounds percussion can produce.

Orchestra Cove

Song visits the Orchestra Cove, where she observes an orchestra in action, learning how different instruments harmonize together. An orchestra is a harmonious blend of diverse instrument families, each contributing its own unique timbre and character to create a symphonic masterpiece. String instruments, including violins, cellos, and double basses, form the backbone with their rich and sustained tones. Woodwinds, such as flutes, clarinets, and oboes, add melodic lines and dynamic expression.

Brass instruments like trumpets and trombones provide powerful, resonant tones, while percussion instruments inject rhythmic vitality. These families, diverse in their construction and sound production, collaborate under the conductor's guidance to achieve a cohesive musical performance.

A conductor explains the role of each instrument family in the orchestra, enhancing Song's understanding. First, the strings, often the largest section, establish the foundation of the orchestra, conveying melody, harmony, and texture. Woodwinds contribute expressive melodies and intricate harmonies, showcasing agility and lyrical qualities.

Brass instruments bring brilliance and grandeur, often used for majestic fanfares or triumphant themes. Percussion, ranging from timpani to a variety of drums and cymbals, punctuates and enhances rhythmic elements, providing color and intensity. The conductor coordinates these families, ensuring a balanced and nuanced performance where each instrument family plays a vital role, contributing to the orchestra's overall sonic palette. The collective synergy of these instrument families results in the breathtaking complexity and emotional depth that define orchestral music.

Song's exploration uncovered the rich tapestry of instrument families. Strings wove emotive melodies, woodwinds danced with lyrical grace, brass heralded grandeur, and percussion added rhythmic vitality. Together, they formed an orchestra, harmonizing diverse tones.

It is important for you to reflect on this orchestral mosaic. Song's journey celebrates the beauty and diversity of musical instruments, a testament to the universal language that unites them in creating symphonies that resonate with the human soul.

At the end of Song's journey, there was a celebration on the isles, showcasing the symphony of instruments and leaving Song with an impression of the beauty and diversity of musical instruments.

Workbook Activity: Instrument Isles

Activity 9: Instrument Families Coloring
Color different instrument families and learn their unique sounds. Connect instruments to create your mini-orchestra.

Go to activity #9 in your workbook.

Activity 10: Draw Your Instrument
Draw your favorite musical instrument and write a fun fact about it.

Go to activity #10 in your workbook.

Chapter 6:

Clef Caves

Let's now journey together into the mysterious Clef Caves, where musical symbols and notation come to life. We are going to decode the language of very basic sheet music and understand the significance of different clefs.

Entering the Clef Caves

Song stands at the entrance of the Clef Caves, filled with anticipation and wonder, as she hears faint harmonies echoing from within. The Clef Caves beckon with an enchanting allure, their labyrinthine passages adorned with glowing symbols and echoing musical notes that seem to dance in the air. Song enters this mythical area with amazement, her curiosity piqued by the possibility of unlocking musical mysteries concealed within the depths.

Guided by a whimsical musical sprite, she sets on an educational odyssey, each step resonating with the harmonies of knowledge. The walls pulse with the vibrancy of her journey, revealing ancient melodies and forgotten rhythms.

The caves become both the backdrop and the gateway, a space where Song must navigate to progress on her adventure, forging a symphony of discovery in the heart of the mysterious Clef Caves.

Interactive Activity: Create Your Cave

To be fully involved in this new adventure, draw what you imagine the Clef Caves look like, using colors or materials that represent the mystery and excitement of learning music notation. This activity will encourage creativity and set an imaginative context for the adventure.

The World of Clefs

Song enters the Clef Caves. Within these mystical Clef Caves, the walls unveil a mesmerizing tapestry of musical symbols, each representing a distinct clef: Treble, Alto, Tenor, and Bass.

These clefs serve as guides to the pitch ranges of musical notes, which are crucial for musicians to interpret and perform compositions accurately.

- **Treble Clef:** The elegant swirls of the treble clef adorn sheet music, signifying high-pitched notes. Found mostly in the upper registers, it guides instruments like the violin and flute, giving them a distinct musical identity.

- **Alto Clef:** Nestled between treble and tenor, the alto clef allocates its space to instruments like the viola. Its centrality enables a broad pitch range, contributing to the rich harmonies of orchestral compositions.

- **Tenor Clef:** Positioned above bass and below alto, the tenor clef accommodates instruments like the cello and trombone. Bridging the gap, it extends the pitch range, adding versatility to musical arrangements.

- **Bass Clef:** Bold and foundational, the bass clef anchors the lower spectrum of musical notes. Instruments like the double bass and tuba find their home here, providing depth and resonance to the ensemble.

The clefs are crucial in defining music's pitch range, acting as signposts on the staff to guide musicians. As Song explores, each clef acts as a portal to a unique sonic realm, showcasing the diverse pitch ranges within the cave. The echoing walls harmonize with these clefs, inviting Song to explore the rich musical spectrum in each cave section.

Song, captivated by the harmonious symbols surrounding her, engages in an interactive challenge within the cave's depths. Each clef on the walls beckons her to decipher its significance, linking it to the corresponding pitch range. As she successfully decodes the musical hieroglyphics, pathways open, unveiling new sections of the cave and expanding her understanding of the diverse world of musical notation.

Decoding Musical Symbols

In a chamber filled with symbols, as she advances, the cave becomes a living manuscript, its walls adorned with musical expression. Song, mesmerized, encounters a visual feast of notes, rests, dynamics, and articulations etched into the rock. Each symbol pulsates with its own unique energy, creating a visual score that guides the performance of an unseen musical masterpiece. These symbols include:

- Notes, the fundamental building blocks of melody, are delicately inscribed in intricate patterns, each carrying its own unique pitch and duration.

- Rests, representing silences in the score, manifest as quiet alcoves, emphasizing the importance of pauses in the musical narrative.

- Dynamics, illustrated with expressive symbols, weave a narrative of volume and intensity across the cave surfaces, guiding performers to crescendo or decrescendo with the natural ebb and flow of the composition.

- Articulations, depicted as nuanced markings, reveal themselves as ornate carvings, conveying the subtleties of touch and phrasing.

These symbols act as guides, dictating the tempo and shaping the emotional structure of the composition. Some of the examples on the cave walls illustrate how a forte marking demands a bold and powerful execution, while a piano marking calls for a delicate touch.

Song, guided by the musical sprite, deciphers these symbols, discovering their power to shape musical expression. Each symbol she encounters becomes a lesson, a visual representation of the language of music imprinted on the cave walls like an ancient educational mural.

Through this visual journey, Song not only explores the caves but also unravels the intricate grammar of musical notation, gaining a profound understanding of how symbols harmonize to guide the enchanting performance of music.

Navigating the Notation Labyrinth

A labyrinth within the caves represents the complexity of reading sheet music; Song must navigate it to progress. Her guide provided tips on reading music, helping Song decode the musical clues that reveal the path through the labyrinth. Here are some tips that can also help you read sheet music effectively:

Understand the basics:

- Learn the basic elements of sheet music, including the staff, clefs, notes, and rests.

- Understand the concept of measures and time signatures.

Learn the staff:

- The staff consists of five lines and four spaces. Notes are placed on the lines and spaces to represent different pitches.

- Treble clef is typically used for higher-pitched instruments, while bass clef is used for lower-pitched instruments.

Memorize note names:

- Familiarize yourself with the names of the notes on the staff. Use mnemonics if needed (e.g., Every Good Boy Deserves Fudge for the lines in the treble clef, FACE for the spaces).

- Practice recognizing notes quickly.

Practice rhythm:

- Understand the different note durations (whole notes, half notes, quarter notes, eighth notes, etc.).

- Practice clapping or tapping out rhythms to improve your sense of timing.

Use mnemonics for ledger lines:

- When notes go above or below the staff, use mnemonics to remember the names of the notes on ledger lines.

Learn key signatures:

- Understand key signatures and how they affect the pitch of notes.

- Memorize the key signatures for major and minor keys.

Practice sight-reading:

- Regularly practice sight-reading to improve your ability to read and play music on the spot.

- Start with simpler pieces and gradually progress to more complex ones.

Use a metronome:

- Practice with a metronome to develop a steady sense of rhythm and tempo.

Break it down:

- Break down the music into smaller sections and practice each section before attempting to play the entire piece.

Learn dynamics and articulation:

- Understand dynamic markings (e.g., forte, piano) and articulation symbols (e.g., staccato, legato) to convey expression in your playing.

Take your time:

- Initially, go at a slower pace to ensure accuracy. As you become more comfortable, gradually increase your speed.

Use apps and online resources:

- There are many apps and online tools designed to help you practice reading sheet music. These can include interactive exercises and games.

Seek feedback:

- If possible, get feedback from a teacher or more experienced musician. They can offer guidance on your reading and interpretation skills.

Remember that reading sheet music is a skill that improves with consistent practice. Be patient with yourself, and enjoy the process of learning and making music!

As she solves notation puzzles, Song (and the reader) gain practical skills in interpreting sheet music.

The Hidden Harmony of the Caves

In a chamber within the Clef Caves, the walls are adorned with intricate compositions, serving as a captivating canvas for Song's education. Here, she delves into the essence of musical notation, discovering how melody, harmony, and rhythm manifest on the staff.

The complex arrangements on the cave walls become a visual symphony, each note and symbol a brushstroke contributing to the grand composition of a musical masterpiece. As Song studies these intricate scores, the cave itself transforms into a living textbook, unraveling the language of music before her eager eyes.

Guided by a mentor, Song learns not only to read the symbols but also to understand their interplay. In a chamber resonant with the magical acoustics of the caves, the guide orchestrates a demonstration, using the environment to showcase how melody, harmony, and rhythm harmoniously converge in music. Song's senses become attuned to the intricate dance of musical elements, enriching her understanding of their combined effect.

Armed with newfound knowledge, Song takes on the challenge of deciphering a specific piece of sheet music. With determination, she identifies the role of each musical element within the composition, weaving together the intricate threads of melody, harmony, and rhythm. The chamber echoes with the triumphant harmony of comprehension as Song unlocks the secrets concealed in the musical notation, marking a pivotal moment in her journey through the Clef Caves.

Interactive Activity

Compose a short piece of music using basic notation. You can draw it on manuscript paper. You should practically apply your understanding of melody, harmony, and rhythm in notation.

In the heart of the caves, Song reviews what she has learned, realizing she can now understand the language of simple sheet music. The guide commends Song for her newfound skills, encouraging her to continue her musical journey. Song is able to leave through the other side of the caves feeling empowered and eager to explore more music, inspiring readers to do the same.

Workbook Activity: Clef Caves

Activity 11: Clef Decoder
Decode basic sheet music symbols and understand the significance of different clefs.

Go to activity #11 in your workbook.

Activity 12: Draw the Notes
Use blank music sheets to draw notes and symbols based on the provided instructions.

Go to activity #12 in your workbook.

Chapter 7:

Dynamics Canyon

Brave the Dynamics Canyon, where the volume of music is a challenge to conquer. You are going to learn about pianissimo to fortissimo and how dynamics add depth and emotion to musical pieces.

Entrance to Dynamics Canyon

Standing at the enigmatic entrance of Dynamics Canyon, Song is captivated by a symphony of sounds resonating with varying intensities from within. Excitement and intrigue course through her veins as a dynamic guide, a character renowned for expressive musical performances, warmly welcomes her. This guide becomes Song's gateway to a musical adventure, delving into the profound world of dynamics. As they step into the canyon, the guide imparts the importance of dynamics in music, emphasizing the interplay of volume and intensity.

The path, shrouded in mist, echoed with ethereal sounds of varying volumes, resonating through the atmosphere with a mystical quality. The entrance exuded an enigmatic aura, both inviting and foreboding, as if the canyon held musical secrets waiting to be unveiled. Song's heart echoed the canyon's dynamics; a mix of excitement and nervousness pulsed within her. She stood at the threshold, ready to explore the nuanced landscapes of musical dynamics—the art of shaping volume and intensity. The canyon seemed to whisper promises of revelations, beckoning Song to embrace the mysterious journey ahead, where the interplay of sounds would unlock the secrets of musical expression.

The Spectrum of Sound

Song goes on an enthralling adventure through an ancient canyon, where she encounters passages and natural barriers that match the dynamic levels of music, ranging from delicate pianissimo to strong fortissimo. The geological formations are a canvas for the expressive language of sound, visually representing the ebb and flow of melodic intensity. Guided on her journey, Song learns the art of manipulating dynamics in music. The guide ingeniously employs the canyon's acoustics, showcasing how variations in volume can transform a musical piece.

With each demonstration, the canyon becomes a living, resonant classroom, echoing the nuanced interplay between soft and loud musical passages. First, she has to learn that music dynamics encompass a vast spectrum, spanning from the barely audible pianissimo to the thunderous fortissimo. In between, she finds the moderate tones of mezzo-piano and mezzo-forte, offering nuanced expressiveness. These dynamic markings guide musicians in conveying the intended emotional intensity of a piece.

In sheet music, dynamics are visually conveyed through symbols and abbreviations, adding a dynamic dimension to the composition. Pianissimo is symbolized by *pp*, suggesting a soft, almost whisper-like volume, while *mp* indicates mezzo-piano, a moderate softness. *mf* represents mezzo-forte, signaling a moderate loudness, and *ff* stands for fortissimo, demanding a powerful, emphatic delivery. The crescendo symbol "<" prompts a gradual rise in intensity, guiding musicians to build momentum and tension. Conversely, the decrescendo or diminuendo symbol ">" indicates a gradual reduction in volume, allowing for nuanced control over the expressive journey within the musical piece.

An example of dynamic representation in sheet music can be found in Beethoven's Symphony No. 5. The iconic four-note motif, initially marked forte, intensifies with a crescendo, creating a powerful, dramatic effect. Similarly, in Debussy's "Clair de Lune," the delicate opening, marked pianissimo, unfolds through a gradual crescendo, revealing the subtleties of dynamic shading in the composition. These markings serve as vital guides, allowing performers to interpret and convey the composer's intended emotional nuances.

Challenged by her guide, Song faces a unique test. She must adapt her singing or playing volume to align with the dynamic markings on the canyon's walls. This challenge deepens Song's understanding of dynamics.

Interactive Activity: Dynamic Labeling

Obtain a simple piece of music that has a corresponding melody, and then label its dynamic markings. This activity will help you enhance your practical understanding of dynamic symbols.

Echoes of Emotion

In a chamber filled with echoing music, Song experiences firsthand how dynamics convey emotions in music. The guide had a big lecture about these dynamics he had to give to Song. She had to understand that composers skillfully utilize dynamics—

variations in volume and intensity—to evoke emotions and amplify the storytelling element in music. Dynamic contrasts play a pivotal role in shaping the narrative, guiding listeners through peaks and valleys of intensity.

For instance, a gradual crescendo can heighten tension, preparing the audience for a climactic moment, while a sudden diminuendo can create a sense of mystery or introspection.

The guide uses examples from famous musical pieces played within the chamber to show how dynamics change the mood and impact of the music. Examining these music pieces provides tangible examples of how dynamics can alter mood and emotional impact. Take:

1. **Vivaldi's "Spring" from The Four Seasons:**

   In the lively and uplifting "Spring," Vivaldi masterfully employs dynamic changes to mimic the natural world. Crescendos and diminuendos imitate the changing seasons, with the piece ranging from vivacious fortissimos to gentle pianissimos, evoking the joy and renewal associated with springtime.

2. **Chopin's Nocturne in E-flat Major, Op. 9, No. 2:**

   Chopin's Nocturne showcases the pianist's ability to convey profound emotions through subtle dynamics. The soft, expressive opening introduces a dreamlike atmosphere, and as the dynamics ebb and flow, the piece weaves a narrative of introspection and longing.

3. **Tchaikovsky's Swan Lake, Act II, No. 10:**

   The dynamic variations in this piece contribute to the emotional depth of the ballet. From the delicate, almost ethereal swan theme marked by pianissimo to the powerful fortissimo moments representing the dramatic elements, the dynamics amplify the contrast between the delicate and the powerful in this iconic composition.

4. **Mozart's Symphony No. 40, Molto Allegro:**

   Mozart's Symphony No. 40 showcases a range of dynamics to convey intense emotions. The bold fortissimo sections create a sense of urgency and drama, while softer dynamics provide moments of reflection. The interplay between these dynamics in the Molto Allegro movement contributes to the symphony's emotional complexity.

By scrutinizing dynamics in renowned compositions, one can appreciate the nuanced storytelling capabilities of composers, recognizing how changes in volume and intensity contribute to the emotional structure of music.

Song listens to different dynamics in music, expresses how each makes her feel, and describes the emotions conveyed through the dynamics in them.

The Dynamics Challenge

A series of challenges within the canyon require Song to use her knowledge of dynamics to proceed, like adjusting volumes to unlock doors. Each challenge demonstrates a practical aspect of dynamics, from subtle changes to dramatic shifts. Song has to apply dynamics in various ways to successfully overcome each of these challenges.

- **Resonant Rocks:**

Song encounters a series of massive, resonant rocks scattered throughout the Canyon. Each rock responds to a specific musical frequency. To progress, she must play notes on her instrument, adjusting the volume and pitch until she discovers the correct combination that resonates with each rock. This challenges her understanding of dynamics as she experiments with different volumes to unlock the harmonic secrets of the environment.

- **Echoing Echoes:**

In a cavern with exceptional acoustics, Song faces the challenge of creating echoes in a precise sequence. She must use her understanding of dynamics to control the intensity and timing of her musical notes. By adjusting the volume and rhythm, Song creates a cascade of echoes that bounce off the canyon walls. The solution lies in mastering the interplay between her instrument's dynamics and the natural acoustics of the environment.

- **Waterfall Sonata:**

Song encounters a stunning waterfall with musical locks preventing her passage. The water's flow responds to changes in volume. Song must play a musical sequence that aligns with the waterfall's rhythm. By adjusting the dynamics of her performance, she manipulates the waterfall's cascading patterns, unlocking new pathways. This challenge not only tests her understanding of dynamics but also requires a keen sense of timing to harmonize with the natural flow.

- **Wind Whispers:**

High above the Canyon, Song faces a puzzle involving wind chimes suspended in the air. Each chime corresponds to a different musical element. By adjusting the volume and pitch of her instrument, Song orchestrates a symphony with the wind, unraveling the secrets hidden in the melodies. This challenge not only requires her to adapt to the dynamic changes in wind speed but also demands a nuanced understanding of how to manipulate her music to interact with the atmospheric elements.

The Whispering Walls and Roaring Passages

Next, Song ventures into regions of the canyon where the dynamics of sound are at extreme opposites. In one area, she discovers a serene, quiet grove, while in another, a roaring waterfall produces deafening sounds.

This stark contrast emphasizes the significant impact of volume in music. Song must adapt her playing style to the surroundings, learning to appreciate how extreme dynamics can evoke different emotions and shape her musical journey through the canyon.

Along her journey, her guide imparts insights into the importance of control and balance in using dynamics effectively. The guide emphasizes how mastering dynamics is not just about playing loudly or softly but about crafting a musical narrative.

Song learns that dynamics are tools for expression, and their judicious use can elevate her performance, creating a more engaging and immersive experience for both herself and any listeners she may encounter in the canyon.

In a secluded area, Song faces challenges that push her to experiment with creating dynamic contrasts. She encounters scenarios where extreme dynamics are necessary to overcome obstacles or unlock hidden passages.

As she grapples with these challenges, she gains a deeper understanding of the nuanced effects of extreme dynamics on the mood and atmosphere of her musical surroundings.

This experiential learning allows Song to develop a heightened sensitivity to when and how to apply dynamic contrasts, enhancing her musical prowess and enriching her exploration of the canyon.

Near the end of the canyon, Song reflects on her dynamic journey, realizing the profound impact of dynamics on musical expression. The guide acknowledges her growth, praising Song's newfound understanding.

Encouraged to persist in exploring dynamics, Song departs the canyon empowered, determined to infuse her music with richer emotional tones.

Her journey serves as an inspiration, urging us to embrace dynamics for a more expressive and captivating musical experience in our own artistic endeavors.

Workbook Activity: Dynamics Canyon

Activity 13: Volume Challenge
Color the canyon based on different dynamic levels, and understand how dynamics add depth to music.

Go to activity #13 in your workbook.

Activity 14: Dynamics Story
Draw a comic strip illustrating a musical story using different dynamic markings.

Go to activity #14 in your workbook.

Chapter 8:

Time Signature Temple

From the Dynamics Canyon, you are to enter the Time Signature Temple, where the rhythm of music is sacred. You will understand time signatures, syncopation, and how they shape the rhythmic structure of a piece.

Welcome to the Time Signature Temple

Song arrives at the majestic entrance of the Time Signature Temple and is intrigued by the patterns and symbols adorning the gateway. A rhythmically inclined guide, perhaps a drummer, welcomes Song and reminds her of the concepts of time signature in music and rhythm. In the grand temple, a musical sanctuary, symbols and harmonious sounds converge to embody the fundamental elements of advanced rhythm, governed by a diverse array of time signatures. Song walks in and is immediately enthralled by the colorful display, which piques her curiosity and causes her initial excitement to surge. Different time signatures provide a distinct rhythm that permeates the atmosphere, each providing a different rhythmic experience. Song's amazement at the variety of ways that musical cadence can be expressed is reflected in the setting, which turns into a kaleidoscope of rhythmic possibilities. A gentle reminder highlights rhythm as the beating heart of music, its pervasiveness forming the compositional framework. It highlights how important rhythm is to the orchestration of a work, serving as a force that defines and directs the ebb and flow and mimicking the complex relationship of the musical elements.

The Secrets of the Temple

Song explores a hall filled with clocks and metronomes, each ticking to a different time signature. This reminded her of time signatures. The guide explains time signatures again, expanding on more of them and demonstrating with the metronomes, helping Song feel and understand the differences. As a reminder, time signatures in music are a crucial organizational framework for beats, dictating the structure and pace of a musical piece. Represented as a fraction at the beginning of a musical score, time signatures convey vital information about the rhythm and meter of the composition.

The top number signifies the number of beats in a measure, while the bottom number designates the note value that receives one beat. This system enables musicians to synchronize their performances, providing a shared understanding of the rhythmic foundation. The common time signatures include the following:

- **4/4 Common Time:** Common time, symbolized by the 4/4 time signature, is the most prevalent in music. Each bar contains four beats, with the quarter note receiving one beat. Its regularity provides a stable and straightforward rhythmic foundation, making it versatile for various genres, from pop to rock.

- **3/4 Waltz Time:** Waltz time is indicated by the 3/4 time signature. It features three beats per measure, with the quarter note receiving one beat. This signature is characteristic of the graceful and rhythmic waltz dance. The rhythmic emphasis on the first beat lends itself to a flowing and lilting feel, creating an elegant and danceable atmosphere.

- **6/8 Compound Time:** In 6/8 time, each measure contains two beats, with each beat made up of three eighth notes. This compound time signature divides beats into two groups of three, fostering a distinct triplet feel. Widely used in folk, blues, and classical music, 6/8 time provides a compound rhythm that feels both intricate and expansive, allowing for creative and syncopated patterns.

Understanding these time signatures provides a foundation for musicians to convey different rhythmic nuances, influencing the overall feel and character of the music they create.

Now, let's try to engage in a rhythmic exploration. In 4/4 time, clap on each of the four beats; switch to a 3/4 waltz time, and feel the shift to a triple meter. Transition to 6/8, where the compound feel encourages a different kind of tapping or clapping.

Further complexity arises when musicians incorporate changes in time signatures within a single piece. This dynamic shift can enhance musical expression and create unique rhythmic textures. As we experience these variations, it becomes apparent how time signatures play a pivotal role in shaping the character and flow of music. So, let's tap along and feel the pulse of diverse time signatures, appreciating the rhythmic diversity they bring to musical compositions.

The Rhythm Patterns Altar

In a chamber adorned with different time signatures, Song learns about how time signatures change note values and how to recognize different rhythms within time signatures. The guide explains everything to her. As you now know, time signatures influence the perceived speed and feel of a composition. Changing the time signature alters the duration and emphasis of notes, impacting the overall rhythm. For instance, switching from 4/4 to 3/4 time transforms the rhythmic feel, creating a waltz-like flow with three beats per measure.

Rhythmic patterns exhibit remarkable diversity, adapting to various musical styles and genres. In common time (4/4), the classic "rock beat" places emphasis on beats two and four, creating a driving feel. Jazz often explores complex syncopations within common time, challenging traditional rhythmic conventions. Odd time signatures, like 7/8 or 5/4, introduce unique rhythmic patterns. Tool's "Schism," for instance, navigates intricate rhythms within 5/4, enhancing the song's progressive and dynamic nature. Time signatures serve as a canvas for musicians to experiment with rhythmic diversity, allowing them to craft intricate patterns that contribute to the overall character and expression of the music.

To construct basic rhythm patterns, start by understanding the time signature and assigning note values accordingly. For instance, in 2/4 time, two quarter notes fill a measure. Recognizing patterns involves identifying recurring rhythmic motifs. Clapping or tapping along helps internalize these patterns. Practice with metronomes enhances precision in rhythm recognition.

You should unleash your creativity by crafting original rhythm patterns within a specific time signature. Experiment with different note values and placements, keeping in mind the beats per measure. This exploration fosters a deeper understanding of rhythmic possibilities and empowers you to contribute your unique voice to the musical landscape.

Syncopation Sanctuary

Song enters a part of the temple where rhythms become more complex, featuring off-beat and syncopated patterns. The guide breaks down the concept of syncopation as a rhythmic technique disrupting regular beat patterns with unexpected accents, and it adds complexity and interest to music. Injecting a dynamic, unpredictable quality, it creates tension and release by emphasizing typically unaccented beats, engaging listeners with unexpected rhythmic twists.

Syncopation defines jazz through its presence in improvisational solos and unpredictable drum accents. In Latin music, particularly salsa and bossa nova, syncopation creates infectious grooves. African and Afro-Caribbean rhythms in Afrobeat and reggae showcase their role in crafting vibrant, danceable patterns.

Significantly shaping rock, pop, and funk, syncopation characterizes the latter with tight, intricate rhythms. Hip-hop relies on it for intricate, compelling beats, while electronic dance music (EDM) leverages syncopation to craft dominant, energetic rhythms on the dance floor. Across genres, syncopation enriches compositions, introducing unexpected accents and enhancing the overall listening experience with its dynamic and unpredictable qualities.

Syncopation is a cornerstone in music, shaping diverse genres. In jazz, think of Miles Davis' trumpet in "So What," where offbeat accents create an unpredictable flow.

Moving to rock, listen to Led Zeppelin's "Good Times Bad Times," where drummer John Bonham's syncopated kick drum introduces a dynamic groove. In hip-hop, syncopation defines the genre, as evident in the intricate beats of Kendrick Lamar's "King Kunta." Even classical music embraces syncopation; Stravinsky's "Rite of Spring" features rhythmic surprises that stir emotions. Across genres, syncopation injects vitality, fostering a sense of unpredictability that defines the unique feel of each musical style.

Song tries out different syncopated rhythms, understanding how they add interest and complexity to music.

Composing with Time

Choosing the right time signatures and rhythm patterns is crucial in music composition. Song discovers the significance of matching time signatures with melodies and genres. The guide provides essential tips on this, emphasizing that certain signatures enhance specific melodies and genres.

To assist Song in grasping the concept practically, the guide provides practical tips. It emphasizes the importance of understanding the distinct feel associated with different time signatures. Effective composition is encouraged by experimenting with contrasting rhythm patterns to discover a unique combination that aligns with the desired emotional tone.

The guide suggests maintaining coherence in a composition either by staying consistent or purposefully introducing breaks for emphasis. Rhythm exercises are highlighted as valuable tools for skill refinement. Starting with simple patterns, composers are advised to gradually introduce complexity to their compositions. The process involves practicing the creation of short musical pieces within a selected time signature, allowing for exploration of various rhythmic possibilities.

Additionally, the guide recommends analyzing existing compositions for inspiration. By studying how renowned composers manipulate time signatures in their work, composers like Song can gain insights into evoking specific emotions. This practical approach encourages hands-on learning, enabling Song to apply theoretical knowledge to her composition process.

By dedicating time to mastering time signatures and rhythm patterns through deliberate practice, composers can unlock a world of creative possibilities, infusing their music with depth, emotion, and individuality.

Guided by the expert, Song listens to how a melody evolves when paired with various time signatures. Recognizing that not all signatures suit every melody, Song gains insights into the nuanced relationship between melody and rhythm.

In a hands-on session, Song chooses a time signature (excluding the conventional 4/4) and revises her melody and rhythm accordingly. The guide assists in refining the composition, ensuring harmony between Song's creative expression and the chosen time signature. This immersive experience equips Song with the skills to thoughtfully incorporate time signatures and rhythm patterns into her future.

Reflecting on her temple journey, Song reflects on key rhythmic concepts she learned. The guide commends her understanding, encouraging further exploration. Leaving the temple, Song, inspired and motivated, heads towards the castle, ready to apply her newfound knowledge in the musical adventure that lies ahead.

Workbook Activity: Time Signature Temple

Activity 15: Time Signature Puzzles
Solve puzzles to understand the concepts of time signatures and syncopation.

Go to activity #15 in your workbook.

Activity 16: Rhythmic Patterns
Create your own rhythmic patterns using the blank sheet provided.

Go to activity #16 in your workbook.

Chapter 9:

Grand Composition Castle

Finally, you have reached the Grand Composition Castle, the heart of Harmonyland. Discover the basics of a full-length musical composition, how to read sheet music in depth with all of the components learned throughout the book, and even try your hand at creating your own musical masterpiece.

Arrival at the Grand Composition Castle

As Song approaches the Grand Composition Castle, its imposing and magnificent presence evokes awe and anticipation. At the culmination of her journey through Harmonyland, she breathes a sigh of relief at overcoming challenges and making it in time for the festival. Each trial has been a lesson, preparing her for this final test. The castle's grandeur symbolizes the magnitude of the musical concepts she's about to face, linking its majesty with the intricate beauty of full-length compositions. At this moment, Song embarks on a journey into the complexities of music, mirroring her own growth. The castle becomes a symbol of her cumulative learning experience, and as she steps inside, trepidation blends with excitement, knowing she's ready to showcase her acquired skills and face the ultimate musical challenge.

Interactive Activity: Castle Sketch

You can make your own Grand Composition Castle, incorporating elements you've learned about music so far, like rhythm patterns on the walls or dynamic markings. Now that you have made all of the parts of Harmonyland, you can put all your drawings together.

Exploring Full-Length Compositions

In the grand journey of musical exploration, the anatomy of a full-length song reveals itself as Song navigates through diverse halls and rooms that represent the spectrum of compositions. These expansive pieces differ markedly from the short melodies and rhythms Song has encountered so far, offering a rich tapestry of musical elements.

As Song explores each room, she encounters historical compositions that showcase motif development, a concept akin to musical storytelling. Motifs are like musical characters that evolve and transform throughout a piece, providing depth and continuity. While discussing these ideas, Song's holographic guides explain how repetition and contrast, like the changing scenes in each room, play vital roles in creating engaging musical narratives.

In the journey through time, Song learns about the evolution of full-length musical pieces. She comes to understand that musical evolution spans from the intricate multiple-movement concertos of the classical era, such as Beethoven's Ninth

Symphony, to the contemporary landscape of today's top 40 hits. Each era contributes distinct styles and structures, showcasing a transition from the formal compositions of the past to the eclectic fusion of genres prevalent in modern music.

From the structured brilliance of Mozart's symphonies to the genre-blending creativity seen in works like Bohemian Rhapsody by Queen, the evolution of full-length musical pieces reflects the dynamic nature of artistic expression, influenced by cultural shifts and technological advancements.

The holographic displays reveal the different layers of production that contribute to today's dynamic and evolving musical landscape. Song gains insight into how the foundations laid by classical masters have influenced contemporary artists, creating a fascinating continuum of musical expression.

Through this immersive journey, Song not only learns about the anatomy of a full-length song but also gains a profound understanding of how musical compositions have transformed and adapted over time, creating a vast and interconnected musical universe.

Mastering Sheet Music

In the musical journey of Song, the narrative unfolds as she enters a room brimming with complex sheet music spanning diverse eras and genres. Fueled by a thirst for knowledge and armed with valuable resources, Song embarks on a quest to decipher the language of music. Her focus sharpens on interpreting more sophisticated rhythms, advanced dynamics, and nuanced articulation symbols that weave through the musical tapestry.

Song's exploration goes beyond individual elements as she unveils the synergies of melody, harmony, rhythm, and dynamics within the intricate lines of sheet music. Sheet music serves as a canvas where diverse elements—melody, harmony, rhythm, and dynamics—converge to craft a cohesive musical narrative. Each element is a brushstroke contributing to the overall masterpiece. Song intertwines with harmony, rhythm dictates the pace, and dynamics shape the emotional landscape. Understanding this interplay is crucial for musicians aiming to interpret and convey the composer's intended message. It's the ability to see beyond individual notes, recognizing the synergy that transforms a mere arrangement of symbols into a captivating musical journey.

As the plot unfolds, Song introduces practical exercises meticulously designed to hone the reader's ability to read and comprehend comprehensive musical pieces. These exercises serve as bridges, connecting the lessons from previous chapters and allowing readers to apply their knowledge in real-world scenarios.

- **Exercise 1: "Harmonic Fusion"**

She combines melodies from different genres and eras, challenging herself to navigate through dynamic changes, intricate rhythms, and varied articulations. This exercise encourages a seamless integration of elements learned in previous chapters, fostering adaptability and versatility.

- **Exercise 2: "Expressive Storytelling"**

She selects a complex musical piece and guides musicians in interpreting it with a focus on storytelling. She emphasizes dynamic contrasts, articulate phrasing, and rhythmic precision to convey the emotional narrative embedded in the composition. This exercise not only tests technical proficiency but also cultivates a deeper connection between the musician and the music.

The Composer's Workshop

In a dynamic workshop setting within the castle, Song immerses herself in the art of crafting and developing musical ideas. Expert composers and holographic guides become her mentors, teaching her techniques to transform embryonic musical concepts into full-fledged compositions. Great songwriters follow these ten tips when composing music and you can too:

- **Craft a catchy melody:** Focus on creating memorable melodies that move in stepwise motion with occasional leaps, incorporating a focal point to anchor the line.

- **Use diverse chords:** Expand your musical palette by incorporating major, minor, dominant, diminished, and augmented chords for a richer sound.

- **Develop a memorable rhythm:** Pay attention to rhythmic motifs, as funky or syncopated patterns can enhance the catchiness of your songs.

- **Build around a riff:** Whether on guitar, piano, bass, or other instruments, anchor your song with a distinctive riff to make it stand out.

- **Design songs for live performance:** Consider how your songs will translate to live performances, as record executives value a musician's connection with live audiences.

- **Write away from your instrument:** Break away from familiar tropes by stepping outside, crafting melodies and rhythms mentally, and later translating them to your instrument.

- **Experiment with song structure:** Challenge yourself to go beyond traditional structures; try incorporating elements like intros, pre-choruses, bridges, and outros to add complexity.

- **Balance lyric-writing structure and spontaneity:** Plan your lyric-writing process but allow room for discovery, letting lyrics come naturally based on ideas, titles, or existing lines.

- **Use rhyme strategically:** Employ rhyme schemes to enhance catchiness and memorability, but don't feel constrained by them—follow the idea rather than forcing rhyme when it's not suitable.

- **Overcome writer's block:** Break through creative blocks by varying your process, trying different orders for music and lyrics, experimenting with new instruments or genres, and stepping outside your comfort zone to spark creativity.

As Song explores the workshop, she engages in discussions on structuring compositions and expanding melodies into full-length pieces. Expert guidance helps Song understand the architecture of a musical composition, including considerations of form, phrasing, and thematic development. The workshop becomes a canvas where Song learns the art of sculpting musical landscapes, ensuring that her compositions resonate with a well-defined structure and narrative flow.

Additionally, the guide unfolds insights into the creative process of composing, incorporating modern digital tools into Song's toolkit. The workshop introduces her to the vast possibilities offered by digital technology, from virtual instruments and synthesizers to digital audio workstations. Song discovers how these tools enhance her creative capabilities, providing avenues for experimentation and innovation. The guides encourage an exploration of the intersection between tradition and technology, emphasizing the seamless integration of digital tools to amplify the creative potential within the composition process.

Crafting Your Musical Masterpiece

In the grandest hall of the castle, Song is tasked with creating her full-length composition, applying all the knowledge she has gained, which she did. She then shared the steps she went through to complete the task. The following are the steps she advises you to follow:

- **Step 1: Establish Constraints for Your Composition**

Begin with a deliberate approach by setting restrictions for your musical creation. Your objective is to compose a piece using only one note, fostering creativity by narrowing down ideas. Discard any notions exceeding two notes, focusing solely on crafting an exceptional single note. Define parameters before sketching:

1. Choose a tempo (e.g., 60 beats per minute).

2. Specify the time signature (e.g., 4/4).

3. Decide on the key signature (e.g., C major).

4. Select the instrument(s) playing the note (e.g., the violin).

Now, with the foundational details in place, move on to the creative process.

- **Step 2: Composing with a Singular Note**

Envision your chosen note without the need to hear it beforehand. Consider its range (high, middle, or low), volume (loud or soft), evolving dynamics, and duration. Picture the note's journey:

You can envision a middle-range, soft note played on the violin. It starts extremely softly, gradually intensifying with each beat. By the third beat, it crescendos to a very loud volume, concluding with a swift acceleration of the bow to produce the resonant sound of an open low G string.

Then, write down your vision: a low G, 3 beats long, starting very soft (*pp*), and getting very loud (*fff*).

You can embark on this musical journey, experimenting with styles and elements to find a unique voice. Whether choosing lyrics or an instrumental approach, the aim is to unleash creativity. Embrace diverse styles, from classical to contemporary, and experiment with rhythm, harmony, and instrumentation to express individuality in the world of music.

The narrative motivates breaking free from conventions, fostering a fearless spirit of musical innovation.

In the final chamber of the castle, Song reviews her completed composition and reflects on both her journey and the process. Song prepares to perform her piece at the festival.

Workbook Activity: Grand Composition Castle

Activity 17: Composer's Workshop
Learn the basics of composing music and try your hand at creating a short musical piece.

Go to activity # 17 in your workbook.

Activity 18: Sheet Music Challenge
Read and interpret a simple sheet music piece using all the components you learned.

Go to activity #18 in your workbook.

Chapter 10:

The Finale Festival

It is time for the Finale Festival, a celebration of everything learned in Harmonyland. First, you will explore different genres of music and a great musician or two from each. Then perform your own musical creation, showcase your newfound knowledge, and watch Song complete her adventure and be crowned the Finale Festival Queen Musician.

The Grand Opening of the Finale Festival

The Finale Festival in Harmonyland bursts with vibrant hues, resonating with the symphony of music and jubilation. The air is alive with anticipation, with every corner adorned with kaleidoscopic decorations, creating a visual feast for the senses. Song, the protagonist, finds herself immersed in this vivacious ambiance, her heart pulsating to the rhythm of excitement that courses through the lively streets.

As the festival reaches its peak, Song stands at the heart of it all, a beacon of the journey she embarked upon in pursuit of musical mastery. Harmonyland, echoing with cheers and melodies, awaits the grand showcase of skills and knowledge, symbolizing the culmination of countless hours dedicated to honing musical prowess.

Amidst the bustling crowd, mentors and guides who once shaped Song's musical odyssey gather at the castle. Their presence not only adds to the festivity but also serves as a testament to Song's growth as a musician. Each note played, every skill showcased, becomes a brushstroke on the canvas of her journey, painting a portrait of triumph and unity in the dazzling tapestry of the Finale Festival.

A Journey Through Genres

Song's journey through the Finale Festival is a kaleidoscopic odyssey, each step revealing a new section dedicated to a specific music genre. The classic section, adorned with ornate decorations, echoes the timeless elegance of symphonies and orchestras. The classical enclave, adorned with ornate decorations, resonates with the timeless elegance of symphonies and orchestras. Originating in the medieval and Renaissance eras, classical music boasts intricate compositions that emphasize harmony and structure. Pioneers like Mozart and Beethoven, with their masterpieces such as "The Magic Flute" and "Symphony No. 9," have eternally shaped the genre, leaving an indelible mark on musical history.

Moving into the jazz realm, bathed in dim, moody lights, Song encounters a space pulsating with improvisation and syncopation. Born in the late 19th and early 20th centuries, jazz evolved from blues and ragtime. Jazz luminaries like Miles Davis and John Coltrane revolutionized the genre with their innovative improvisations, immortalized in albums like "Kind of Blue" and "A Love Supreme."

The rock section exudes raw energy, featuring iconic guitar riffs and rebellious anthems. Originating in the mid-20th century, rock evolved from blues and country. The Beatles, with their groundbreaking "Sgt. Pepper's Lonely Hearts Club Band," and Jimi Hendrix, known for his electrifying guitar skills in "Purple Haze," reshaped the musical landscape with their revolutionary contributions.

In the pop area, vibrant colors and catchy tunes dominate, reflecting the genre's mainstream appeal. Originating in the 1950s, pop music emphasizes accessibility and widespread popularity. Icons like Michael Jackson, the King of Pop, and Madonna, the Queen of Pop, have left an enduring legacy with chart-topping hits like "Thriller" and "Like a Virgin."

Finally, the folk section, adorned with rustic charm, resonates with storytelling and acoustic simplicity. Rooted in oral traditions, folk music celebrates cultural narratives. Influential figures like Bob Dylan, with his socially conscious lyrics in "Blowin' in the Wind," and Joan Baez, a folk icon, have influenced generations with their profound contributions.

As Song immerses herself in each genre, she discovers the rich tapestry of music's evolution, its diverse voices echoing through time, transcending boundaries and genres.

Song's Musical Showcase

As the Finale Festival approaches its zenith, Song finds herself engrossed in meticulous preparation for her grand performance. The air buzzes with excitement, and the vibrant festival atmosphere only amplifies her anticipation. Wandering through the festival grounds, she stumbles upon an invitation card that adds a layer of significance to the event—the annual Musician Queen pageant. This is a tradition where everyone casts their votes for a musician who best embodies passion and dedication to learning. This card sends a shiver down Song's spine. The realization that she, too, could be a contender for the coveted title ignited a spark within her.

The prospect of being recognized not just for her musical prowess but also for her unwavering commitment to the art fills her with a mix of nerves and exhilaration. As Song delves into the complexity of her performance, she can't help but reflect on the journey she has undertaken since her arrival in Harmonyland.

From the tentative notes played in the early days to the complex compositions she is now mastering, the progress is palpable. Each challenge, every mentor, and every setback has sculpted her into the musician she has become.

The resonance of her growth echoes in the chords she practiced, a testament to the countless hours spent honing her craft. Amidst the rehearsed notes and timed pauses, Song finds herself reminiscing about the mentors and guides who have shaped her musical odyssey.

Their encouragement, critiques, and shared passion for music still echo in her mind, serving as both motivation and a reminder of the musical community she has become a part of.

As Song fine-tunes her performance, she marvels at the vast distance she has covered. The festival, now not just a celebration of music but a potential platform for recognition, symbolizes the culmination of her journey. With every note, she pours not just melody but also her journey's essence, hoping to resonate not only with the audience but also with the spirit of the Musician Queen pageant—an embodiment of passion and perpetual learning.

The Grand Performance

The moment arrives under the twinkling festival lights as Song steps onto the grand stage, her instrument cradled in her hands like an extension of her being. The hushed anticipation of the audience heightens as she positions herself, a lone figure against the backdrop of the festival's dazzling colors.

As Song begins to play, her fingers dance across the instrument with newfound dexterity and confidence. The music that emanates isn't just a sequence of notes; it is a manifestation of her journey—the highs and lows, the challenges overcome, and the knowledge acquired. The performance seamlessly weaves through different genres, a testament to her diverse learning experiences in Harmonyland.

In the classical segment, she showcases precise articulation and emotional depth, the echoes of Mozart and Beethoven reverberating through her melodies. Transitioning to jazz, her improvisational skills take center stage, the notes bending and weaving in spontaneous harmony, a nod to the jazz legends who had inspired her. Rock follows suit, the stage pulsating with the raw energy of her electric guitar.

With a cascade of powerful chords and infectious rhythms, she pays homage to the rock icons who have shaped her musical identity

The pop segment is a celebration of catchy tunes and infectious beats, a reflection of the genre's universal appeal. Song seamlessly integrates folk elements, her acoustic strumming resonating with authenticity and storytelling. The audience is enraptured by the rich tapestry of sounds, each genre flawlessly interwoven, showcasing her ability to traverse the musical spectrum effortlessly.

As the final notes linger in the air, thunderous applause erupts from the audience. The once-hushed atmosphere transforms into a symphony of cheers and appreciation.

Song, bathed in the warmth of the spotlight, feels a profound connection with the crowd. The smiles, the tears, and the standing ovation are not just acknowledgments of her performance but affirmations of the collective musical journey she has undertaken.

The festival goers, moved by the depth and diversity of Song's performance, sense that something extraordinary has unfolded on that stage. Song, with her newfound skills and knowledge, has not just played music; she has woven a musical tapestry that resonated with the hearts of all who listened—an ode to the transformative power of passion and perpetual learning.

Interactive Activity: Home Concert and Reflection

Perform the piece you've composed for your family or friends and reflect on the experience as you go through Song's journey and the different hands-on experiences through the interactive activities.

Song's Coronation and Farewell

Under the luminous festival lights, the crowd erupts in cheers as Song, with tearful eyes and a heart brimming with gratitude, is crowned the Finale Festival Musician Queen. The tiara sparkles on her head, a symbol of her remarkable achievement and the recognition of her passion for music.

The applause is a thunderous symphony, resonating with the shared joy of the musical community.

As Song stands on the stage, crowned and beaming, she feels not only the weight of the tiara but also the responsibility it carries. The title is not just a culmination but a commencement—a proclamation that her journey is merely the overture to a lifelong musical adventure.

With a humble acknowledgment, Song knows that the crown signifies not just her accomplishments but also the promise to continue learning, growing, and sharing the magic of music with the world.

Workbook Activity: Finale Festival

Activity 19: Musical Genre Showcase
Explore different musical genres and color a musical collage showcasing your favorites.

Go to activity #19 in your workbook.

Activity 20: Grand Finale Performance
Perform your own musical creation, showcasing your newfound knowledge.
Crown Song as the Finale Festival Queen Musician!

Go to activity #20 in your workbook.

Dear Reader,

I hope Jane Vera's stories have brought a little more joy, wonder, and imagination into your world. I'd love to hear how the book made you feel and what parts sparked your curiosity. Your feedback means the world to me, and it helps others discover the magic of storytelling too.

Leaving a review might seem like a small thing, but it makes a huge difference! It helps more readers find my books and inspires me to keep creating new stories. Plus, I read every single review—yes, each one! Knowing what you loved (or even what you'd like to see more of) helps me grow as an author.

If you have a moment, I'd be so grateful if you could share your thoughts online. Thank you for being part of this journey with me!

With gratitude,
Jane Vera

Conclusion

Congratulations, young musician! You've completed the extraordinary Musical Quest and emerged as a certified Harmonyland Hero. As your guide, Song the Musical Explorer, it's my honor to present you with a prestigious musical diploma—a testament to your dedication, curiosity, and unwavering passion for the magical world of music.

Let's reflect on our journey, revisiting the major lessons from each chapter of the Musical Quest. Together, we ventured through the Rhythm Kingdom, where beats and notes danced to their own tune. Here, you learned about note values, time signatures, and the heartbeat that underlies all music—a foundation for understanding the rhythmic intricacies of any musical piece.

Next, we strolled through the enchanting Melody Forest, where tunes and melodies grew on musical trees. Exploring scales, intervals, and the art of creating your own musical melodies, you discovered the secrets that bring life to compositions, offering a melody-rich landscape to harmonize your musical expressions.

Climbing the Harmony Hills, you gained insights into chords, harmony, and the delicate art of blending different musical notes to create harmonious sounds. The trek through the Tempo Desert challenged you to understand the unpredictable speed of music—tempo and dynamics—shaping the mood and intensity of every musical journey.

Sailing to the Instrument Isles, you met the diverse musical inhabitants playing a variety of instruments. This chapter illuminated the families of instruments, their unique sounds, and how they harmoniously unite in an orchestra—a symphony of different voices contributing to the grand musical narrative.

Journeying into the mysterious Clef Caves, you deciphered the language of sheet music and explored the significance of different clefs. The Dynamics Canyon challenged you to master the volume of music, from the softest pianissimo to the most powerful fortissimo, adding depth and emotion to your musical palette.

Entering the Time Signature Temple, you discovered the sacred rhythm of music— understanding time signatures and syncopation, crucial elements shaping the rhythmic structure of any musical piece. Finally, you reached the pinnacle of Harmonyland—the Grand Composition Castle. Here, you delved into the basics of full-length musical composition, decoding intricate sheet music, and even trying your hand at creating your own musical masterpiece. Joining the Finale Festival, a celebration of all you've learned, you explored different genres of music and met great musicians who left their mark on each.

Then, you took center stage to perform your own musical creation, showcasing your newfound knowledge, much like Melody completing her adventure and being crowned the Finale Festival Queen Musician.

Your journey mirrors mine, as Song the Musical Explorer, and that of countless musicians who find joy, solace, and inspiration in the enchanting world of music. The musical diploma you now hold is not just a certificate; it's a key to a universe of possibilities. You are a Harmonyland Hero, equipped with the knowledge to traverse the vast landscapes of music, explore its nuances, and create your unique melodic story.

Now, let's imagine me handing you your well-deserved diploma. Picture it—a parchment adorned with musical notes, a seal of accomplishment, and my signature, Song the Musical Explorer. It symbolizes your mastery of the Musical Quest and the boundless potential that lies ahead on your musical adventure.

As your guide and fellow explorer, I encourage you to continue your musical exploration and practice. Your journey is just beginning, and the world of music awaits your unique contribution. Cherish the melodies that resonate with your soul, embrace the challenges that refine your craft, and let your passion guide you through the symphony of life.

Remember, the magic of music is boundless, and with your diploma in hand, you are equipped to create, explore, and make your mark on the musical landscape. Congratulations, Harmonyland Hero! May your musical journey be as vibrant and fulfilling as the melodies you've uncovered and shared throughout this enchanting quest.

References

A complete guide to music clefs: What are they and how to use them. (2018, August 22). Musicnotes. https://www.musicnotes.com/blog/a-complete-guide-to-musical clefs-what-are-they-and-how-to-use-them/#:~:text=A%20music%20clef%20is%20a%20symbol%20that

Aichele, M. (2018, August 8). *Understanding time signatures and meters: A musical guide.* Liberty Park music. https://www.libertyparkmusic.com/musical-time-signatures/

Ben. (2013, January 18). *Dynamics forte, piano, and crescendo, all explained.* Music Theory Academy. https://www.musictheoryacademy.com/how-to-read-sheet-music/dynamics/

Benefits of music & nature connection. (2014, September 16). Natural Musicians. https://www.naturalmusicians.co.uk/why-make-music-and-connect-with-nature/

BRUNOTTS, K. (2022, April 20). *How to harmonize vocals: The complete guide.* Emastered. https://emastered.com/blog/how-to-harmonize-vocals#:~:text=Find%20Your%20Root%20Note

Brunotts, K. (2021, November 27). *How to write a melody: The complete beginner's guide.* Emastered. https://emastered.com/blog/how-to-write-a-melody

Cantan, N. (2017, March 2). *How to teach time signatures (the Fun Way) in the Piano Studio.* Colorful Keys. https://colourfulkeys.ie/how-to-teach-time-signatures-the-fun-way-piano-studio/#:~:text=Relative%20Rhythms

Genres. (n.d.). School-learning zone. https://school-learningzone.co.uk/key_stage_two/ks2_music/musical_genres/genres.html

George, G. S. (n.d.). *Time signatures explained: the common and not-so-common ones.* Piano Blog by Skoove - Piano Practice Tips. https://www.skoove.com/blog/time-signatures-explained/

Guide to the Orchestra. (n.d.). The Kennedy Center. https://www.kennedy-center.org/education/resources-for-educators/classroom-resources/media-and-interactives/media/music/guide-to-the-orchestra/

Hamm, C. (2021). Reading clefs. Viva pressbooks. https://viva.pressbooks.pub/openmusictheory/chapter/clefs/#:~:text=One%20mnemonic%20device%20that%20may

Learn about harmony in music. (n.d.). Music Theory Academy. https://www.musictheoryacademy.com/category/understanding-music/harmony/

How do musicians know how fast to play a piece? And why are the terms in Italian? (n.d.). Symphony nova scotia. https://symphonynovascotia.ca/faqs/symphony-101/how-do-musicians-know-how-fast-to-play-a-piece-and-why-are-the-terms-in-italian/#:~:text=Andante%20%E2%80%93%20at%20a%20walking%20pace

How to compose music: A step-by-step guide for songwriters. (2021, November 16). Better Songs. https://bettersongs.com/how-to-compose-music/

How to read sheet music: A step-by-step guide. (2014, April 11). Music notes. https://www.musicnotes.com/blog/how-to-read-sheet-music/

Hutchinson, R. (n.d.). *Common rhythmic notation errors*. Music theory. Retrieved January 9, 2024, from https://musictheory.pugetsound.edu/mt21c/CommonRhythmicNotationErrors.html#:~:text=Syncopation%20occurs%20when%20notes%20on

Icon Collective. (2020, August 24). *Basic music theory for beginners: The complete guide*. https://www.iconcollective.edu/basic-music-theory

Instruments—Dallas Symphony Orchestra. (2020, November 7). Dallas symphony. https://www.dallassymphony.org/community-education/dso-kids/listen-watch/instruments/

Kiss, B. (n.d.). *How to use a metronome*. Free Online Metronome. Retrieved January 9, 2024, from https://www.metronomeonline.com/how-to-use-a-metronome

Lavoie, A. (2019, November 22). *What is rhythm: How time, beat and meter work in music*. LANDR Blog. https://blog.landr.com/what-is-rhythm-time-beat-meter/

Lessons. (2019). Music theory. https://www.musictheory.net/lessons

Luis. (2023, March 10). *Three-part-harmony*. Signaturesound. https://signaturesound.com/three-part-harmony/#:~:text=It%20is%20important%20to%20understand

M, A. K. (2023, August 24). *The power of melody and harmony: How music evokes emotion*. Medium. https://medium.com/@athilk25/the-power-of-melody-and-harmony-how-music-evokes-emotion-82693f4b7bf3#:~:text=The%20Language%20of%20Melody%20Pitch%20and%20Intervals:

Music for kids: How brass instruments work. (n.d.). Ducksters. https://www.ducksters.com/musicforkids/how_brass_instruments_work.php

Music for kids: How string instruments work. (n.d.). Ducksters. https://www.ducksters.com/musicforkids/how_string_instruments_work.php#:~:text=All%20stringed%20instruments%20make%20sound

Music for kids: How woodwind instruments work. (2019). Ducksters. https://www.ducksters.com/musicforkids/how_woodwind_instruments_work.php

Musical instrument facts for kids. (n.d.). Kids.kiddle. https://kids.kiddle.co/Musical_instrument

Nuzzolo, M. (n.d.). *Music mood classification | Electrical and computer engineering design handbook*. https://sites.tufts.edu/eeseniordesignhandbook/2015/music-mood-classification/#:~:text=Faster%20tempos%20are%20associated%20with

Percussion instruments. (2023, October 27). Classics for Kids. https://www.classicsforkids.com/percussion-instruments/

Pouska, A. (n.d.). *Time signatures*. StudyBass. Retrieved January 9, 2024, from https://www.studybass.com/lessons/reading-music/time-signatures/#:~:text=The%20top%20number%20of%20the

Syncopation facts for kids. (2019). Kiddle. https://kids.kiddle.co/Syncopation

Team, S. (n.d.). *5 tips for learning to read music for the beginning string musician*. Connolly music. https://www.connollymusic.com/stringovation/5-tips-for-learning-to-read-music-for-the-beginning-string-musician

The beat goes on: Understanding the fundamentals of rhythm In music. (2023, February 16). IMusician. https://imusician.pro/en/resources/blog/fundamentals-of-rhythm-in-music

The harmonics of nature. (2022, December 12). The Harmonics of Nature. https://harmonicsofnature.com/

(2024). Twinkl. https://www.twinkl.ca/teaching-wiki/four-families-of-the-orchestra

Made in United States
Troutdale, OR
05/08/2025

31184884R00055